Naxos travel guide

2024-2025

Discover the Timeless Beauty and Hidden Treasures of Naxos

George Smilo

Copyright Notice for "Naxos Travel Guide" by George Smith

© [2024] George Smith. All rights reserved. Except for brief quotations included in critical reviews and certain other noncommercial uses allowed by copyright law, no part of this publication may be reproduced, distributed, or transmitted in any form or by any means, including photocopying, recording, or other electronic or mechanical methods, without the author's prior written permission.

TABLE OF CONTENTS

INTRODUCTION.. **6**
CHAPTER ONE : Overview of Naxos................ **12**
    Brief History..12
    Geography and Climate................................. 16
    Capital charm... 20
CHAPTER TWO: GETTING THERE..................**24**
    Transportation Options..................................24
    Airports and Ferries..28
    Local Transportation..................................... 34
CHAPTER THREE : ACCOMMODATION........... **40**
    Hotels..40
    Villas and Vacation Rentals.........................44
    Budget Options... 50
CHAPTER FOUR: EXPLORING NAXOS TOWN (CHORA).. **58**
    Archaeological Museum................................58
    Portara... 64
    Old Town (Kastro)... 69
    Venetian Museum... 75
CHAPTER FIVE: BEACH GUIDE......................**80**
    Agios Prokopios... 80
    Plaka... 84
    Agia Anna..88
    Mikri Vigla...92
CHAPTER SIX: HISTORICAL SITES.................**96**
    Temple of Apollo...96

Kouros of Melanes.. 100
Bazeos Tower..104

CHAPTER SEVEN: ACTIVITIES AND ADVENTURE..106
Hiking Trails... 106
Windsurfing and Kiteboarding....................... 110
Scuba Diving.. 115

CHAPTER EIGHT: LOCAL CUISINE..................120
Traditional Naxian Dishes............................. 120
Popular Restaurants...................................... 124
Food Festivals..128

CHAPTER NINE :NIGHTLIFE AND ENTERTAINMENT... 134
Bars and Clubs...134
Cultural Events...136
Folklore Evenings..140

CHAPTER TEN: SHOPPING............................ 144
Local Markets...144
Souvenirs... 148
Art and Handicrafts....................................... 152

CHAPTER ELEVEN:DAY TRIPS...................... 158
Small Cyclades.. 158
Apollonas Village...161
Filoti Village... 165

CHAPTER TWELVE:PRACTICAL INFORMATION. 170
Currency and Banking..................................170
Local Customs... 173

Emergency Contacts......................................178
CHAPTER THIRTEEN: USEFUL TIPS..............184
Best Time to Visit... 184
Packing Essentials....................................... 188
Safety Tips... 193
CONCLUSION..200
Recap of Highlights......................................203
Farewell to Naxos... 207

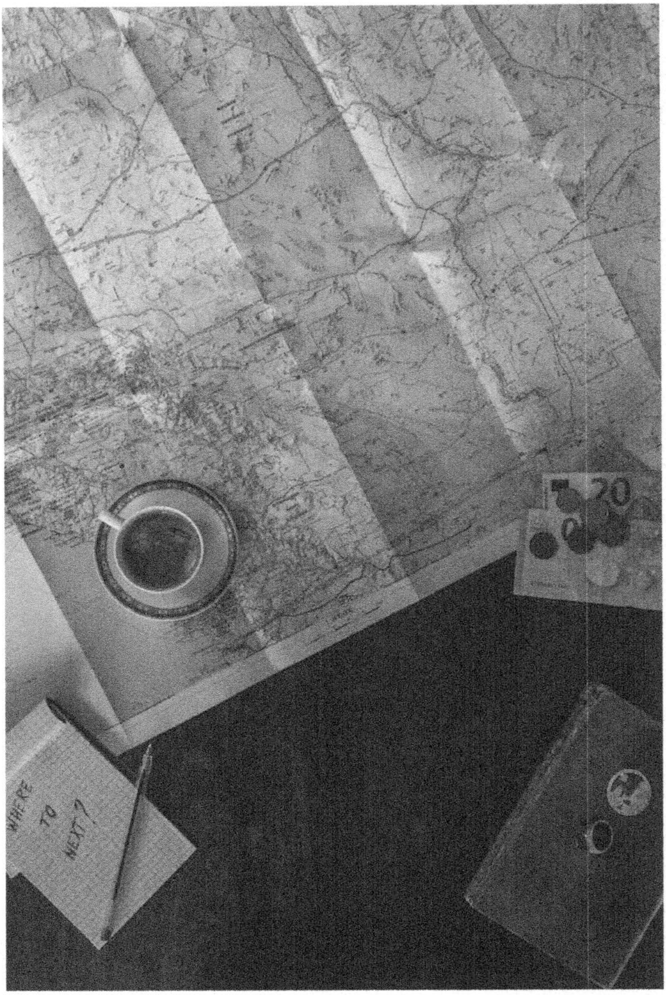
WHERE
TO
NEXT?
20

INTRODUCTION

Welcome to Naxos, the biggest gem in the Aegean crown, where modernism and antiquity mingle and golden beaches are embraced by blue waves. This all-inclusive travel guide extends an invitation to go on an enthralling voyage throughout an island enshrouded in legend, embellished with historic marvels, and graced by the gentle embrace of the Cycladic sun.

Exploring Naxos: A Multicultural Tapestry

The largest island in the Cyclades, Naxos, invites visitors to discover its fascinating history, indulge in the beauty of immaculate beaches, and sample the flavors of genuine Naxian food as it reveals its tapestry of varied landscapes. This charming location, tucked away in the Aegean Sea, beckons with a tasteful fusion of old world charm and modern sophistication.

The Chronicle of Choro: A Visit to Naxos Town

Our trip starts in Naxos Town, also known as Chora, which features an amazing fusion of Cycladic and Venetian architecture. Explore the maze-like passageways of the medieval Old Town (Kastro), where whitewashed walls reverberate with stories of past civilizations.

Admire the Portara, a historic marble entrance that frames the blue horizon and provides a window into Naxos' legendary past.

Sandy Shores and Turquoise Waves: Beach Bliss

Explore the charm of Naxos' beaches as the island comes to life, from the bustling Agios Prokopios shoreline to the serene Plaka and Agia Anna. Take a dip in glistening clear seas, relax on powder-soft beach, and listen to the Aegean sea wind murmur tales of seafaring exploration.

Temples, Towers, and Kouros Statues: Ancient Echoes

Naxos' historical sites are weighted by millennia of history. Discover the Temple of Apollo, where the enormous Portara guards the dreams of the past. Explore Melanes's Kouros statues and take in the ruins of a more innocent time. Naxos's historical story is given a contemporary twist by the Bazeos Tower, a cultural refuge.

Awaiting Adventure: Trekking Paths and Water Wonders

Naxos provides hiking routes that wind across breathtaking scenery for people looking for adventure. Take to the waves in Mikri Vigla for windsurfing and kiteboarding, or explore the depths of the Aegean for scuba diving.

Enjoying Naxos: Regional Flavors and Culinary Delights

Naxian food honors regional ingredients and cooking customs. Take a culinary voyage that reflects the island's abundance of agricultural products, from the tartness of Kitron liquor to the savory joys of traditional cuisine.

Come along with us as we explore the center of Naxos, finding undiscovered treasures, appreciating the lively local culture, and making lifelong memories. With this book, you may discover the beauties of Naxos, where every sunlit beach and cobblestone walkway offers an amazing experience.

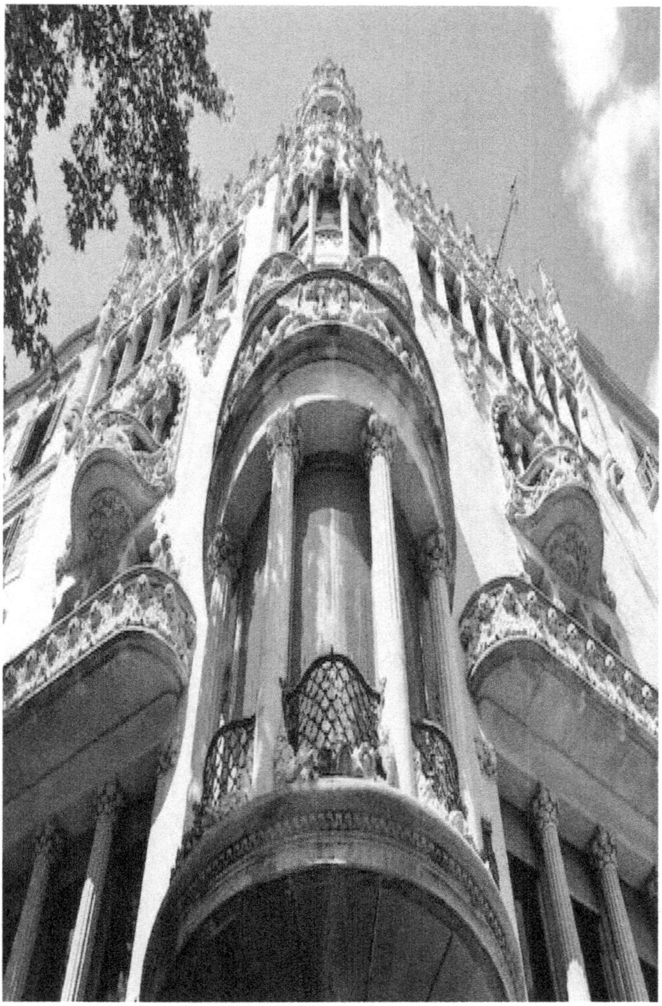

CHAPTER ONE
:Overview of Naxos

Brief History

Naxos History: An Aegean Tapestry of Civilization

The largest island in the Cyclades, Naxos, has a rich millennium-long history. Naxos' historical narrative unfolds as an engrossing tale of cultural evolution, from ancient myth to classical antiquity and the echoes of numerous civilizations.

Myth and Legend of Prehistoric Naxos

Naxos is one of the most important figures in mythology. Zeus, the king of the gods, is said to have grown up in the Naxos highlands. The island's old scenery has a mythological quality due to its association with the stories of Dionysus and Ariadne. Greek mythology's significance for Naxos lays the groundwork for its historical relevance.

Classical and Archaic Eras: Naxos as a Cultural Center

The Cycladic civilization first settled on Naxos in the third millennium BCE, and they left behind marble sculptures as artifacts of their culture. The island demonstrated economic wealth through its marble quarries and was a member of the Delian League during the Archaic and Classical periods.

Portara and the Temple of Apollo: Architectural Wonders

Dating back to the sixth century BCE, the Temple of Apollo is one of the island's most recognizable sites. The temple is yet incomplete, but its imposing Portara entrance stands boldly on the islet of Palatia. This enormous marble gateway facing the sea is evidence of Naxos's aspirations in the past.

Medieval and Byzantine Times: Empire Rule

Naxos endured invasions and pirate incursions during the Byzantine era, experiencing the ups and downs of power. The island was ruled by the Venetian Duchy of Naxos in the thirteenth century. The Kastro (castle) and the medieval neighborhood in particular exhibit strong Venetian architectural influences.

Ottoman Domination and Emancipation: Ages of Change

In the sixteenth century, Naxos joined the Ottoman Empire during the Ottoman era. The island did not regain its independence until the Greek War of Independence in the beginning of the 1800s. Naxos' history was significantly changed by the liberation, which brought the island into line with the recently established Greek state.

Culture, Agriculture, and Tourism in Modern Naxos**

The economy of Naxos saw changes in the 20th and 21st centuries. Historically well-known for its farming, especially the production of citrus fruits, olives, and grapes, the island is today a popular travel destination. Its charm as a diverse tourism destination is enhanced by its historical landmarks, cultural events, and immaculate beaches.

Final Thought: An Evolving Chronicle

The laughter of contemporary beachgoers mingles with the murmurs of old myths, presenting Naxos as a living history. The island's ageless allure is enhanced by its history, which is replete with episodes of wealth and adversity, cultural exchanges, and the rise and fall of civilizations. Discovering Naxos is a trip through the eras that shaped this extraordinary jewel in the Aegean Sea, not just via geographical settings.

Geography and Climate

Naxos's Geography and Climate: The Aegean's Masterpiece of Nature

The largest island in the Cyclades archipelago, Naxos, invites visitors to see its natural wonders all year round with its enthralling tapestry of varied landscapes and Mediterranean temperature.

Diversity in Geography: Plains, Mountains, and Coastal Attractions

With an area of about 429 square kilometers, Naxos has a varied geography that includes lush lowlands, gorgeous beaches, and mountainous areas. Mount Zas, the tallest summit in the Cyclades, is located in the center of the island and provides sweeping views of the surrounding Aegean Sea. Naxos's agricultural wealth is accentuated by valleys and plains, especially in the central and southern districts, while a rocky coastline offers a striking contrast.

Naxian Beaches: Golden Sands and Turquoise Waters

Numerous beaches, each with a distinct appeal of its own, line the island's shoreline. Plaka entices with its tranquil beauty, Agia Anna offers relaxation along its golden sands, and Agios Prokopios greets guests with a bustling atmosphere. Every choice can be satisfied by Naxos' diverse coastline, whether you're looking for quiet coves or exciting seaside activities.

Climatic Conditions: Mediterranean: Sunny Summers and Mild Winters

The Mediterranean climate that Naxos enjoys is warm and dry in the summer and pleasant and rainy in the winter. The island's warmest months are June through September, when long, bright days are ideal for outdoor recreation and beach exploration. Winter, which lasts from December to February, brings with it intermittent rainfall and colder temperatures that turn the terrain into a verdant meadow.

Springtime Blossoms and Autumn Calm: Off-Peak Peace

A new beauty can be seen in the spring and fall, when the island is covered in golden hues and the landscapes are adorned with flowering wildflowers. For those looking for a more relaxed vacation, these shoulder seasons offer a peaceful environment that is perfect for hiking, exploring local culture, and soaking up the ambiance.

Wind Patterns: A Watersports Playground

Especially in the summer, Naxos is renowned for its consistent Meltemi winds, which are ideal for kiteboarding and windsurfing. In the southwest, Mikri Vigla has grown to be a popular destination for swimmers looking for exhilarating moments on the Aegean waves.

Recap: Naxos: A Naturalist's Dream Come True

Naxos is essentially a climatic and geographical symphony that suits a wide range of preferences. Every season invites exploration and discovery, and this island, with its rocky peaks of Mount Zas, sun-drenched beaches, and cultural embrace of Naxos Town, is a nature lover's dream come true. In the center of the Aegean, Naxos continues to be a work of natural beauty, whether it is exposed to the strong summer sun or the soft spring and fall breezes.

Capital charm

Chora, or Naxos Town, is shown as a fascinating center that skillfully combines culture, history, and coastal charm. Tucked away on Naxos' western shore, this Cycladic treasure begs visitors to meander through its winding lanes and discover stories of Venetian influence, historic wonders, and modern vitality.

Castle Kastro: An Iconic Medieval WorkThe Kastro, the center of Naxos Town, takes visitors back in time. This ancient district is a maze of narrow lanes that lead to lovely squares and hidden corners embellished with archways covered with bougainvillea. The Kastro's old churches, museums, and charming stores are all worth exploring because of its timeless splendor.

Portara: The Eternal Entrance to NaxosThe Portara, an iconic representation of the island's long-standing ambitions, stands proudly at the entrance to Naxos Town. This enormous marble entrance, which was formerly a part of an incomplete temple honoring Apollo, creates a striking scene when set against the Aegean Sea.

The Portara turns into a silhouette when the sun sets, creating a mystical ambiance that is filled with the hushed recollections of bygone eras.

Attractive Waterfront: Naxos HarborA hint of maritime appeal is added by the harbor of Naxos Town, where yachts and fishing boats gently sway against the backdrop of the Venetian stronghold. With their expansive views of the sea and the islet of Palatia, where the Portara keeps guard, seaside promenades beckon strollers to take their time.

Cultural Treasures: Bazeos Tower and MuseumsThe cultural treasures of Naxos Town highlight the island's rich history. The Archaeological Museum reveals ancient relics that shed light on the historical significance of Naxos. A cultural hub, the Bazeos Tower, brings a contemporary touch with shows, concerts, and other events honoring regional and global innovation.

CHAPTER TWO: GETTING THERE

Transportation Options

Naxos Transportation Options: Getting Around the Aegean Jewel

To easily visit its varied landscapes, historical monuments, and coastline delights, Naxos, the largest island in the Cyclades, offers a range of transportation alternatives. Every traveler's demands are met by the transportation system, from getting to the island to going about.

1. Ferry Services: Cycladic Gateway Attraction by Sea: Naxos is a key hub in the Cyclades and is well-connected by ferry services. Ferries offer traditional and fast options for a picturesque voyage across the

Aegean, departing from Athens (Piraeus) and other nearby islands.

2.In-country Travel: Aviation Entry to Naxos Airport Naxos: There is an airport on the island that serves domestic travel. For those looking for a quicker route from Athens or other major Greek towns to Naxos, this offers an option. The airport is easily accessible from Naxos Town.

3.Local Transit: Island Exploration Busses: Naxos Town has a large transportation network that links it to other villages, beaches, and island attractions. Buses are a dependable and reasonably priced mode of transportation that let visitors see both well-known and lesser-known locations.

Orientation: There are plenty of taxis in Naxos Town and other important areas of the island.

They offer a practical choice for anyone seeking greater freedom and seclusion when traveling.

Car and Bike Rentals: There are plenty of rental bikes and automobiles available so you can take your time exploring Naxos. For those who desire the freedom to explore the island's interior, find undiscovered jewels, and take beautiful drives, this choice is very intriguing.

4.Rent a Boat: Coastal Discovery Individual Charters: Private boat rentals offer an option for a more individualized experience, enabling visitors to see remote beaches, neighboring islets, and the untamed coastline. For those who want to get away from the throng and take in the peace and quiet of the Aegean, this is the ideal choice.

5.Cycling and Walking: A Relaxed Tour of Towns That Welcome Pedestrians: The pedestrian-friendly nature of Naxos Town and nearby smaller towns encourages leisurely strolls through quaint squares, historic sites, and little alleyways.

Traversing Routes: For those who would rather explore the island on two wheels, there are bicycle routes available. Renting a bike is an eco-friendly and health-conscious way to explore Naxos' natural beauties.

6. Day Trips & Excursions: Activities Outside of Naxos Boat to Adjacent Islands: A convenient starting point for day journeys to nearby islands, such as the Small Cyclades, is Naxos. Regular ferry services provide chances for island hopping and exploration.

Travelers can customize their journeys to fit their interests on Naxos, whether they arrive by ferry, enjoy the scenery from a local bus, or discover hidden jewels by renting a car. Naxos's extensive and well-connected transit system invites exploration from the sea to the mountains, from the historic ruins to the sandy coasts.

Airports and Ferries

Aegean Gateway to Island Bliss: Naxos Airport

The island's airport, which is conveniently close to Naxos Town, is a crucial conduit that connects Naxos to Athens and other important Greek towns. Naxos Airport, with its emphasis on domestic flights, provides guests with an easy and quick method to go to this Cycladic paradise.

1.Modern Comforts and Facilities Terminal Amenities: Even though it's a little airport, Naxos Airport offers tourists the necessities, such as a comfortable waiting area, vehicle rental services, and a cafe for refreshments.

Automobile Rentals: The airport is home to several car rental companies, making it simple for guests to pick up a vehicle when they arrive and tour the island at their own speed.

2.Transportations to Naxos: Linking the Aegean Islands Inner Links: Athens International Airport is the main domestic flight hub for Naxos Airport. For those wishing to connect to and from the Greek capital, these flights provide a practical and expedient choice.

Time of Year Flights: The airport operates on a seasonal basis, with more flights occurring during the busiest travel seasons, which are usually in the spring and early fall.

3. Accessibility for Transportation to and From the Airport, Taxi Services: There are plenty of taxis at the airport that offer a simple and quick ride to Naxos Town or other locations on the island.

Concealed Transactions: Private transfer alternatives are also available, providing comfort and convenience straight to lodging, for those looking for a more individualized experience.

Naxos Ferries: The Cyclades' Maritime Lifelines

Naxos is ideally situated in the center of the Cyclades archipelago, with a strong ferry network connecting it to nearby islands and the Greek mainland. As marine lifelines, ferries offer a picturesque and engrossing way to take in the Aegean's natural splendor.

Navigating the Aegean Blue with Ferry Services

1.Route Naxos-Piraeus: Naxos is connected to the Greek mainland via ferry from Piraeus, the city of Athens' principal port. A popular option for those looking for a relaxing marine experience, the voyage offers stunning views of the Aegean.

   - **Opportunities to Visit Islands:** An ideal starting point for island hopping excursions is Naxos. Frequent ferry services link the island to nearby Cycladic locations, including Mykonos, Paros, Santorini, and other locations.

2. Ferry Types: Comfort and Speed Traditional Ferries: These bigger ships provide a cozier and more leisurely ride. They frequently have features that let guests take use of the sea wind, like lounges, cafes, and outside deck areas.

- **High-Speed boats:** Offering a faster link between Naxos and other islands, high-speed boats cater to individuals who desire faster travel times. These boats are perfect for productive island-hopping trips.

3.Naxos Port and Accessibility: Ferry Terminals Port Naxos: Located in the center of Naxos Town lies the major ferry port. Because of its central location, passengers arriving or departing by ferry may readily reach it.

Fields of View: With amenities like cafes, waiting lounges, and ticket booths, Naxos Port makes sure that travelers are comfortable while they wait for their ship.

4. Reservations and Schedules: Organizing Your Trip** - **Ticketing:** Tickets for ferries can be bought at the port, online, or through travel agents. To guarantee desired travel dates during busy seasons, reservations should be made well in advance.

Timetables: Seasons affect ferry schedules; more frequent services are offered during the busiest travel period. Timetables can help travelers organize their trips more efficiently.

Naxos extends a warm welcome to guests arriving by air or boat, providing a smooth transition from mainland Greece or nearby islands to its coasts. Travelers may completely tailor their tour of this Cycladic beauty by selecting the form of transportation that most suits their tastes, thanks to the airport and boat links.

Local Transportation

Naxos offers an efficient local transportation system that enables visitors to easily explore the island's ancient landmarks, beaches, and quaint villages. This is made possible by the island's varied landscapes and abundance of attractions. There are options to suit different tastes, ranging from buses to taxis, rental cars, and even leisurely walks.

1. Bus: Linking Naxos Town and Surrounding Areas _ Central Bus Terminal: The central bus station is located in Naxos Town and acts as a transportation center for both residents and tourists. From here, the island's numerous communities, beaches, and landmarks are connected by a vast bus network.

Customary Paths: Regular routes are served by buses, which offer a cost-effective and environmentally responsible way to see

Naxos. Popular beaches like Agios Prokopios and Plaka are among the destinations; inland settlements like Filoti and Apiranthos are also worth seeing.

2. Demand and Convenient Taxi - Available Instantly: There are plenty of taxis in Naxos Town and other important areas of the island. Taxis are available for travelers to find at designated taxi stands or to hail on the street.

Comfort and Flexibility: Taxis provide a more private and adaptable form of transportation. When visiting places off the usual road, they are especially perfect for individuals who appreciate straight paths.

3. Car and Bike Rentals: Self-Guided Touring - Car Rentals: In Naxos, there are a lot of car rental companies that provide visitors the opportunity to go about the island on their own. Rental automobiles are particularly useful for traveling to far-flung locations and taking beautiful drives.

Riding Bikes: There are bike rentals available for a more environmentally conscious and energetic experience. Cycling paths may be found across Naxos, enabling cyclists to bike through scenic settings and explore at their own leisure.

4. Traveling by Foot and Walking: A Relaxed Approach- Towns That Welcome Pedestrians: The pedestrian-friendly nature of Naxos Town and nearby smaller towns encourages leisurely strolls through quaint squares, historic sites, and little alleyways.

Trails for Hiking: Hiking trails connect picturesque vistas, historic villages, and archaeological sites around Naxos. Hiking enthusiasts can use their feet to discover the island's historical richness and natural beauty.

5. Rent a Boat: Coastal Excursions - Custom Charters: Private boat charters are offered for anyone wishing to experience the coastline of Naxos from a different angle. These let visitors enjoy the pristine Aegean waters, discover nearby islets, and gain access to secret coves.

6. Day Journeys and Adventures: Traveling Outside of Naxos - Ferry Services: Ferry services provide chances for day visits to nearby islands, while their primary use is for inter-island transportation. For a change of scenery, travelers can venture to neighboring resorts or visit the Small Cyclades.

7. Utilitarian Advice: Optimizing Local Transit - Bus Timetables: Examine bus schedules ahead of time, particularly if you intend to visit particular locations. Schedules can change, so be sure you plan appropriately.

Car Rentals and Taxis: Compared to isolated locations, Naxos Town often has a greater selection of taxis and rental cars. In the high season, think about making reservations in advance.

Walking Around: Take in Naxos' beauty by going on foot explorations. It's best to explore many of Naxos Town's and the villages' attractions on foot.

Local transportation choices in Naxos offer a convenient and flexible experience, allowing each visitor to customize their journey to their own tastes. Navigating around Naxos is an essential part of the island experience, whether you choose the freedom of a rental car, the beautiful route via bus, or the convenience of a taxi.

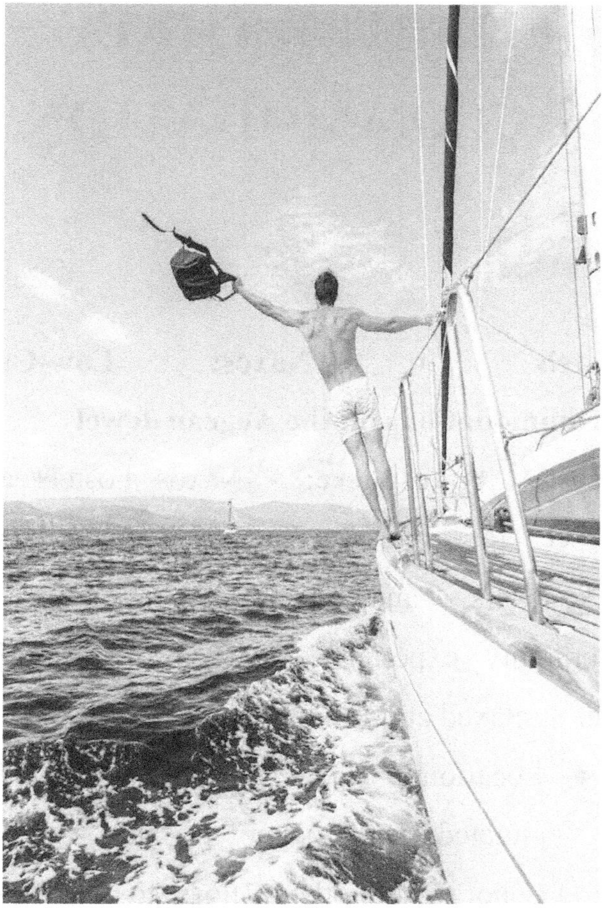

CHAPTER THREE :ACCOMMODATION

Hotels

Hostels in Naxos: Low-Cost Accommodations on the Aegean Jewel

1. Hostel Atmosphere: - Naxos hostels are perfect for tourists on a tight budget, backpackers, and those looking for a community experience because they usually offer a relaxed and friendly atmosphere.

- Location:- Naxos hostels are ideally situated, with some in Naxos Town (Chora) and others close to well-liked beaches or tourist destinations. Naxos Town's central location makes it simple to go to restaurants, transportation, and cultural attractions.

- Types of Accommodation:- Hostels in Naxos often offer dormitory-style rooms with shared amenities and bunk beds. For people who want more privacy, certain hostels may also have private rooms available.
- Facilities:- Standard amenities frequently comprise shared kitchens where visitors can cook for themselves, gathering places for conversation, and Wi-Fi. Bigger hostels may have extra features like laundry rooms and scheduled events.
- Social Events: - To promote a feeling of community among visitors, a lot of hostels in Naxos arrange social events, outings, or group activities. This can be a fantastic opportunity to meet other tourists and go around the island with them.

- Local Recommendations:- The personnel at the hostel are usually happy to offer helpful recommendations for the greatest beaches, eateries, and cultural attractions in the area. They can help with transportation arrangements and tour bookings.
- Booking Platforms:- Well-known internet booking services provide a range of options for hostels in Naxos. You may learn more about the ambiance and services that each hostel offers by reading reviews left by other visitors.
- Seasonal Availability:- Note that the season has an impact on the availability of hostels in Naxos. It's best to make reservations in advance, particularly during the busiest travel seasons.

- Economical Lodging: - Naxos hostels are well-known for offering affordable lodging alternatives, which makes them a well-liked option for tourists trying to maximize their savings while taking in the Aegean's natural beauty.
- Transportation Accessibility:– Most Naxos hostels provide good access to the island's transportation centers, allowing visitors to easily visit ferry ports, bus stops, and airports.

Make sure the hostel you select fits your tastes and travel schedule by always reading the most recent reviews and ratings on reputable booking websites. With its combination of breathtaking scenery and cultural diversity, Naxos is a great setting for shared, inexpensive hostel experiences.

Villas and Vacation Rentals

Naxos Villas & Vacation Rentals: Personalized Getaways in the Aegean

Vacation rentals and villas in Naxos, with its charming appeal and varied scenery, are available for those looking for a more individualized and private experience. These lodging options provide visitors wishing to fully experience the beauty of the Cyclades a place to call home away from home, whether they are tucked away in charming villages or perched on seaside hillsides.

1.Categories of Lodging:
- Homes: Villas on Naxos are large, frequently opulent, and range from classic stone homes to contemporary

masterpieces. Typically, they have beautifully landscaped gardens, private pools, and breathtaking views of the surrounding areas.

- Flats: Holiday apartments, which are frequently found in Naxos Town or close to well-liked beaches, provide a more affordable but nevertheless cozy alternative. They offer a cozy ambiance that is appropriate for families as well as couples.
- Cabins and Residences: Standalone residences or cottages provide seclusion while preserving the originality of regional architecture for those seeking a more private experience.

2. places:

- retreats by the beach: With direct access to the blue waves of the Aegean Sea and expansive views of the coastline, several villas and vacation rentals in Naxos are located right on the beach.
- Village Hideaways:Guests can experience local life, traditional architecture, and the peaceful rhythms of village existence by staying in quaint villas in inland villages like Filoti, Apeiranthos, or Halki.
- Slopeside Getaways: Beautiful views of the island's scenery can be seen from villas located on the hillsides. These lofty hideaways offer a tranquil environment, frequently accompanied by invigorating ocean breezes.

3. Features:

- Separate Swimming Pools: Private pools are a common feature of homes, providing a cool haven in the heated Aegean weather.
- Completely Furnished Kitchens: Many vacation apartments have fully functional kitchens, enabling visitors to cook using local, fresh foods from Naxos' markets.
- Entertainment and Wi-Fi: Modern conveniences like satellite TV, Wi-Fi, and entertainment systems are frequently offered, guaranteeing that visitors are occupied and connected while visiting.

4. Cultural Accents:
- Classic Style: Certain villas use classic Cycladic design elements, such as whitewashed walls, wooden furniture, and regionally produced textiles, creating an atmosphere reminiscent of Greece.

- Crafts and Art from the Area: To give visitors a sense of Naxian culture, the owners frequently adorn their lodgings with handcrafted goods from the area.

5. Booking Sites:
- Virtual Platforms: Travelers can search through possibilities, read reviews, and book their dream villa or vacation rental in Naxos via a number of online booking platforms.

6. Attention to Seasons:
- High Season: It is best to make reservations in advance, particularly from spring through early autumn when demand for these lodgings is highest.
- Off-Peak Offers: In low season, rates can be more reasonable, and vacationers can

get great bargains on villas for a more laid-back and economical stay.

7. Experiences from the Local Area:
- Host Services: Additional services offered by several villas include recommendations, excursion planning, and cultural insights from their local hosts.
- Gastronomic Adventures: To give their guests the opportunity to enjoy real Naxian food, some villa owners provide cooking classes or personal chefs.

Naxos villas and vacation rentals provide a special fusion of opulence, seclusion, and cultural immersion. These lodging options provide a customized getaway for individuals wishing for an exceptional experience in this Cycladic paradise, whether they are tucked away in historic villages, with a view of the azure Aegean, or surrounded by the island's natural beauties.

Budget Options

Economic Lodging on Naxos: Reasonably Priced Comfort in the Aegean

Naxos offers a range of reasonably priced lodging choices, making it a destination that appeals to budget-conscious tourists. These accommodations, which range from quaint guest houses to reasonably priced hotels and hostels, offer a pleasant starting point for island exploration without going over budget.

1.Pensions and Guesthouses:
- Local Charm:In the center of towns or close to the ocean, guesthouses and pensions in Naxos frequently radiate the warmth and charm of the local

community, offering a genuine experience.
- Competitive Prices: Because of their affordable prices, these lodgings are a desirable choice for tourists on a tight budget who want a cozier atmosphere.

2. Cheap Hotels:
- Prominent Locations: Strategically situated in Naxos Town and other important places, low-cost hotels in Naxos offer quick access to dining establishments, transportation, and cultural attractions.
- Prime Features: These hotels provide a comfortable stay with necessary services and sanitation, even though they provide more basic amenities.

3. Studios and Flats:

- Available for Self-Catering: For those on a tight budget who would rather cook for themselves, apartments and studios are perfect. Many have kitchenettes so that visitors can make their own meals using ingredients from the area.
- Flexible Stays: Whether a traveler is staying for a few days to enjoy some exploration or a longer stay, short-term rentals offer flexibility.

4. Hostels:
- Dorms That Are Affordable: Hostels in Naxos provide affordable lodging in the form of dormitories, promoting a social atmosphere perfect for lone travelers or those wishing to meet other adventurers.
- Community Areas: Common rooms and communal kitchens provide guests the chance to socialize and exchange stories.

5. Grilling:

- Camping Locations: Naxos has campsites where visitors can set up tents or park campervans for an even more affordable experience. This is the ideal choice for anyone who wants to be more in tune with nature.
- Areas of Interest: Campsites offer a distinctive opportunity to see the island's surroundings because they are frequently located in picturesque areas.

6. Booking Websites:

- Online Booking Platforms: A plethora of low-cost lodging options in Naxos are displayed on several online booking platforms. Visitors can look through reviews to find lodging options that suit their tastes.

- End-of-Day Offers: Look for last-minute offers, which can provide further savings on inexpensive lodging, particularly during off-peak seasons.

7. Recommended by Locals:
- Ask Locals: Asking around for recommendations from residents or lodging providers may reveal hidden treasures that aren't always highlighted on the internet.
- Away from the Beaten Path:Examining less frequented locations may unveil inexpensive choices concealed in quaint nooks of the island.

8. Benefits of Traveling Off-Peak:
- Low-Season Benefits:Budget-conscious tourists can experience Naxos with fewer crowds and more reasonable pricing by

visiting during the low season, which is typically fall and winter.

9. Consideration of Amenities:
- Standard Comfort: Even though they might not have as many amenities as upscale lodgings, cheap hotels frequently offer the essential comforts for a comfortable stay.
- Real-World Experiences: A more genuine experience can be had by staying at less expensive lodging, which enables visitors to interact with the local way of life.

With its friendly environment and diverse scenery, Naxos guarantees that travelers on a budget will have an enjoyable time without sacrificing comfort. Affordable lodging options abound on this Aegean jewel, whether you choose to stay in a vibrant hostel, a cheap hotel, or a family-run guesthouse.

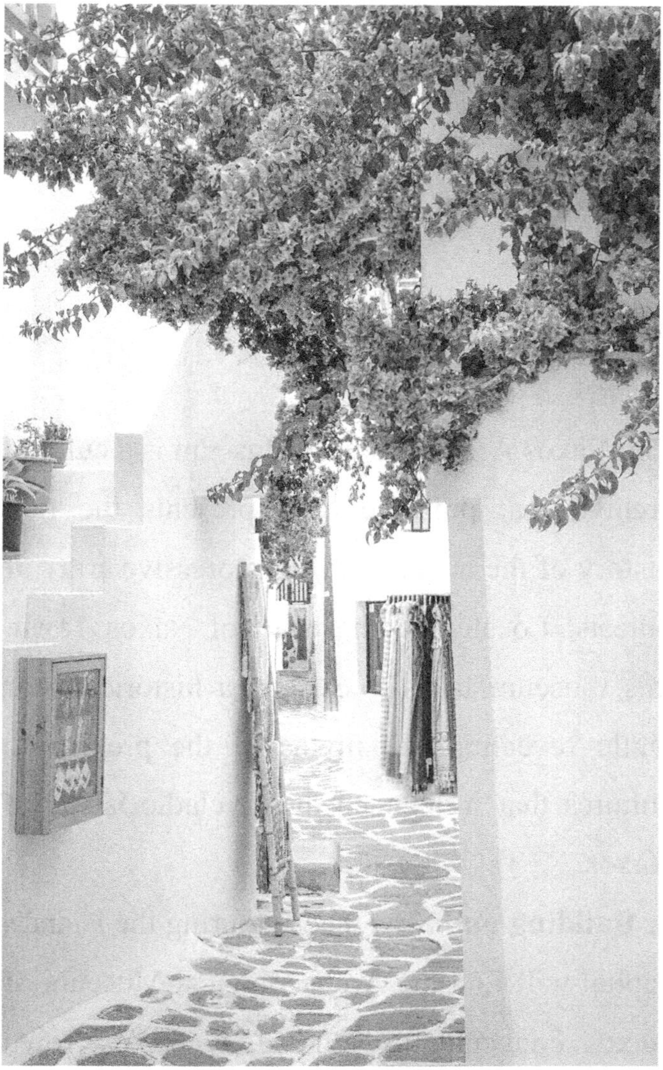

CHAPTER FOUR: EXPLORING NAXOS TOWN (CHORA)

Archaeological Museum

The Naxos Archaeological Museum is a cultural archive that preserves and presents the rich history of the island with an impressive array of objects. Located in the heart of Naxos Town, this museum takes guests on a historical tour while revealing the myths of the prehistoric cultures that influenced the Cycladic island of Naxos.

1. Building and Site: Those touring the island's capital will find the Archaeological Museum of Naxos conveniently situated in Naxos Town (Chora).

- Classic Architecture: The museum itself, housed in a neoclassical edifice, is an architectural marvel that blends well with Naxos Town's traditional atmosphere.

2. Cycladic Civilization: -Historical Context: The museum's displays mostly highlight the Cycladic civilization, highlighting the island's contribution to the formation of this antiquated way of life.

- Chronological Span: The artifacts cover a broad range of historical periods, from the Early Cycladic (3rd millennium BCE) to the Late Roman (late Roman era).

3. Highlights of the Exhibition:- Marble Statues: The Cycladic civilization's marble figurines are a noteworthy collection housed in the museum. These recognizable sculptures, distinguished by their minimalist and abstract forms, provide a window into the creative expressions of the prehistoric occupants.

- Clay and Pottery Artifacts: There are numerous pieces of pottery on show, such as vases and clay objects. These objects illustrate the Cycladic people's everyday lives and craftsmanship.
- Inscriptions and Sculptures: A view into the changing artistic styles and cultural influences on the island can be had by visiting the museum, which is home to sculptures, inscriptions, and reliefs from various historical periods.

4. Importance of the Displays:- Spiritual Relics: A few displays focus on religious objects, providing insight into the spiritual customs of the prehistoric Naxians. These could be figurines, offerings, or items used in religious ceremonies.

- Funerary Objects:Artifacts related to the afterlife, such tombstones and funeral offerings, help shed light on historical burial practices and beliefs.

5.Experience in Education: Through interesting exhibitions, teaching panels, and interactive displays, the museum provides an educational experience. Gain a deeper comprehension of the archeological significance of Naxos.

6.Transient Displays:- Swathes of Collections: Periodically, the museum holds temporary exhibitions that enable a dynamic display of supplementary objects or themes associated with the history of the island.

7. Educational Programs and Guided Tours:-
Guided Tours: There are guided tours that offer deep insights into the historical background and collections of the museum. Experienced tour leaders augment the tourist experience by providing background information and anecdotes about the items.

- Academic Initiatives: The museum may host lectures, workshops, or educational activities to pique visitors' interest and help them develop a greater understanding of the archaeology of Naxos.

8. Practicals for Visitors: - Hours of Operation: Checking the museum's opening hours is advised, as they could change depending on the season.

- Admission costs: If there are any entry costs, they are usually fair. Certain visitor demographics, such elders or students, can be eligible for discounts.

9. Area of Interest Nearby: - Distance from Landmarks: With its prime location in the heart of Naxos Town, the Archaeological Museum is frequently in close proximity to other notable sites, making it simple for guests to include it in their sightseeing plans.

10. Input to Culture:- Maintaining Cultural Heritage: The Naxos Archaeological Museum is essential to the preservation of the island's cultural legacy since it advances academic study and raises public understanding of the historical significance of Naxos.

A trip to the Naxos Archaeological Museum provides an in-depth understanding of the island's history and enables history buffs, academics, and inquisitive tourists to recognize the lasting influence of Naxos and its contributions to the larger picture of Cycladic culture.

Portara

The Portara, an architectural wonder and iconic emblem that unites the island's rich historical past with the present, dominates the skyline of Naxos. Situated on the Palatia islet, a short distance from Naxos Town, this enormous marble entryway evokes the spirit of antiquity and stands as a timeless reminder of the island's enduring past.

1. Historical Importance: - Prehistoric Ruins:The Portara marks the entryway of an incomplete temple erected in honor of Apollo in the sixth century BCE. The temple's imposing entrance, or propylaea, is a stunning reminder of past ambitions even though the temple itself was never finished.

- Historical Relevance: The mythological tales of Theseus and Ariadne are connected to the Portara, so goes the local mythology. The god Dionysus met and fell in love with Ariadne in the Portara, where it is supposed that Theseus left her behind on Naxos.

2. Where and How to Get There: Situated on the islet of Palatia, the Portara is connected to Naxos Town via a causeway. Owing to its elevated location, it offers expansive views of the town, the sea, and the surroundings. Because of the islet's handy proximity to Naxos Town, tourists visiting the capital will find it simple to go to the Portara.

3. Building Elements:- Gigantic Marble Entryway: At over 6.1 meters in height and 3.4

meters in width, the Portara is a gigantic marble gateway. Its enormous size and timeless style highlight the ability and workmanship of the builders of antiquity.

- Underdeveloped Temple: Only the entryway was built, despite the temple's planned dedication to Apollo. Historians continue to conjecture about why it was left incomplete.

4. Sunset Views:- Aesthetic Beauty in Photos: The Portara is especially well-known for its magnificent sunset vistas. Warm colors flood the marble edifice as the sun sets, producing an enthralling and picturesque spectacle.

- Importance in Culture: When the sun sets over the ancient background at the Portara, locals and tourists alike congregate to observe the sky's shifting hues. The sunset has evolved into a social and cultural event.

5. Cultural Occasions:- Musical Events and Exhibitions: The distinct atmosphere of the Portara is used as a location for cultural activities, such as plays and concerts. A captivating environment is created for cultural gatherings when modern art is combined with ancient ruins.

6. A Practical Guide for Guests: - Socks: It's best to wear comfortable shoes, especially if you plan to explore the rocky areas surrounding the Portara.

- Time: Although many people arrive at sunset, the location is equally fascinating during the day. Visitors are free to select a time that best suits their tastes for illumination and crowd density.

- An Historical Analysis: Informational materials and guided tours can enrich the experience by offering historical background and stories related to the Portara.

7. Aegean Sea Panorama: - Surrounding Landscapes: The Portara is a great place for anyone who wants to feel a connection to both history and environment because it provides a panoramic view of the Aegean Sea in addition to views of Naxos Town.

8. Island Symbol:- Symbolism and Legacy: An enduring emblem of Naxos, the Portara symbolizes the island's historical significance and adds to its unique identity.

- Icon of Tourism: Beyond its significance as an archaeological site, the Portara has come to represent Naxos and has attracted tourists from all over the world who come to see its magnificence.

A trip to the Portara of Naxos is an adventure into the ageless stories of mythology, architecture, and the enduring fascination of this Cycladic island, in addition to an examination of ancient ruins. The Portara keeps guard, bridging the gap between the past and the present, as the sun sets over the Aegean.

Old Town (Kastro)

Kastro, or Old Town, Naxos: A Tapestry of Culture and History
Kastro, or Old Town, Naxos, is a living example of the island's rich historical fabric. Inside historic walls, Kastro reveals charming little lanes, Byzantine churches, Venetian architecture, and an air of timeless beauty that draws in tourists. Discovering Kastro is similar

to entering a maze where each stone reveals a fact from bygone eras.

1. Medieval Citadel: Historical Significance: The word "Kastro" alludes to the medieval fortress that formerly defended the island's citizens against pirate incursions. The island's strategic significance is evoked by the remains of the old defenses, which include sections of the defensive wall.

- Venetian and Byzantine Influences: The architecture of Kastro demonstrates the island's historical transition between many civilizations by fusing Byzantine and Venetian elements.

2. Building Wonders: - Mansions in Venice: The small streets of Kastro are lined by Venetian villas covered with vibrant bougainvillea, affording a glimpse into the island's aristocratic history. Numerous of these homes have been painstakingly maintained and remodeled.

- Statue of Couros: A massive statue of Kouros, standing close to Kastro's entrance, connects Naxos to its Greek heritage. The historical sculptural traditions of the island are exemplified by this incomplete statue.

3. Castle Complex:-Venetian Castle (Kastro): The Venetian Castle, a focal point with expansive views over Naxos Town and the surrounding Aegean Sea, is located in the center of Kastro. The Saint Nicholas Cathedral and the Naxos Archaeological Museum are located within the castle complex.

- Saint Nicholas Cathedral: Located inside the castle walls, the cathedral is a focal center for religious and cultural events and has stunning Venetian architecture.

4. Art Galleries and Cultural Centers: - Museum of Archeology: The Archaeological Museum of Naxos, housed within the castle, offers insights into the Cycladic, Mycenaean, and Classical eras through objects from the island's rich past.

- History Museum: The Folklore Museum, which is situated in Kastro, displays traditional clothes, household goods, and agricultural implements to provide visitors with a fuller understanding of Naxian traditions and regional customs.

5 .Secular Structures: - Myrtidiotissa Church of Panagia: Nestled within Kastro, this Byzantine church has stunning architectural elements and frescoes. It serves as evidence of the religious legacy of the island.

- St. Thomas the Apostle: Within Kastro, another religious treasure that showcases the island's multitude of cultural influences is the Saint George-focused Catholic Cathedral of Naxos.

6. Festivals and Cultural Events: - Kastro Festival: Held inside the fortress, the Kastro Festival honors artistic, musical, and cultural events. This yearly festival draws both locals and tourists by bringing the historic surroundings to life.

- Celebrations of Religion: Kastro holds a number of religious events that give the place a more traditional and spiritual feel. Festivals such as Panagia Myrtidiotissa bring pilgrims and participants from across the island.

7. Cafés and Taverns: - Intriguing Places: Kastro's winding lanes are dotted with quaint cafés, boutiques, and tavernas. Taste authentic Naxian food, sip Greek coffee, and peruse regional handicrafts while visiting.

8. Panoramic Views: -Scenic Vistas: Climbing Kastro's winding lanes affords sweeping views of the harbor, Naxos Town, and the blue Aegean Sea. From this high elevation, sunset views are especially charming.

9. Residences in the Area: - Private Nature: Kastro is a neighborhood with local homes as well as a museum. Experiencing the genuine essence of a community that is closely bonded to its environment is possible for tourists who meander around its streets.

10. A Practical Guide to Exploration: - Comfy Shoes: It's best to explore Kastro in comfortable shoes because the cobblestone streets might be bumpy.

- Time of Exploration: Give yourself plenty of time to explore Kastro because every turn offers up surprising views and architectural elements that are hidden treasures.

Kastro, the Old Town of Naxos, welcomes guests to take an enthralling trip back in time. This Cycladic island offers a profound and comprehensive experience where the sounds of ancient civilizations, medieval fortifications, and vibrant contemporary life peacefully blend together.

Venetian Museum

The Venetian Museum, which is situated at the north entrance of the Kastro, is one of such buildings.

The 800-year-old Della Rocca family Venetian home serves as the museum. Entering the mansion gives you the opportunity to live in Venetian style, making it feel like a walk through time. The residence of Mr. Della Rocca's ancestors was transformed into a museum and made accessible to the public. Additionally, he runs the museum entirely on visitor fees without support from the Greek government.

The forty-minute tour is offered in both Greek and English. The length permits a guided tour of the entire home, including the reception hall, bedrooms, dining room, nursery, gallery, library, chapel, study, and balcony with a beautiful view of the harbor of Naxos and the Portara. After that, you are led down to the vaults where you may see authentic artwork from the Venetian era, including paintings, sculptures, pottery, photos, and jewelry.

A visit to the cellars, where you can sample fine wine and other regional beverages, marks the conclusion of the enchanted journey. In addition, you can purchase genuine linens, furniture, and tableware from the rear room as a keepsake of Naxos' Venetian past.

The home also features a lovely, peaceful garden that is a suitable setting for a number of nightly outdoor musical performances. On Wednesday and Sunday evenings, local musicians and dancers dressed in traditional costumes perform a variety of musical styles, including classical, jazz, and traditional Naxos music. There are occasionally performances by international performers as well. If there is one thing you do not want to miss, it is highly recommended that you choose a day when there is a musical concert.

Overall, the Venetian museum gives you insight into the lives of the island's Catholic rulers as well as an understanding of how they shaped Naxos's people and culture. Furthermore, nothing enhances the experience like real music with a real vibe. It is an experience in and of itself, instructive and incredibly enjoyable.

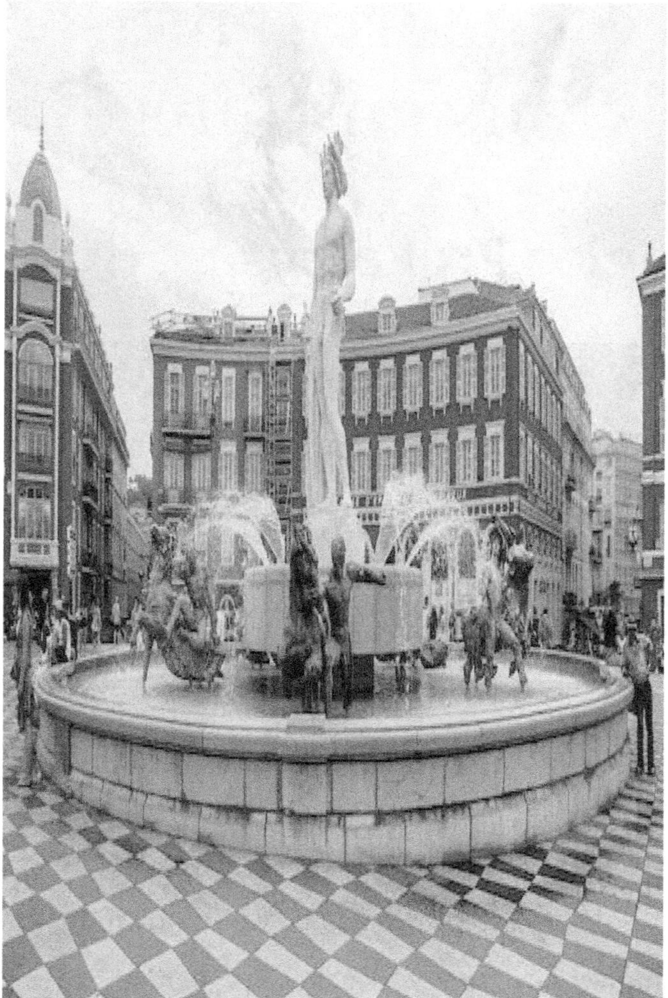

CHAPTER FIVE: BEACH GUIDE

Agios Prokopios

Located on the western coast of Naxos, Greece, Agios Prokopios Beach is well-known for its immaculate sandy beaches, glistening waves, and lively environment. This is a detailed description of Agios Prokopios Beach

1. Golden Sand: Beachgoers are drawn to Agios Prokopios because of its beautiful golden sand, which provides a pleasant and inviting surface. The wide beach offers plenty of room for several kinds of activities as it spans down the shore.

2. Waters That Are Crystal Clear: The beach features pristine turquoise seas that are perfect for snorkeling and swimming. It is appropriate for guests of all ages, from families with young children to those who like water sports, due to its moderate slope into the sea.

3. Water Sports: Agios Prokopios Beach offers a variety of water sports activities, including windsurfing, paddleboarding, and jet skiing. The availability of water sports facilities offers choices for novices and seasoned participants alike.

4. Blue Flag distinction: The beach has been granted the esteemed Blue Flag distinction, signifying exceptional safety standards, environmental consciousness, and great water quality. This endorsement strengthens the appeal of Agios Prokopios as a premier beach resort.

5. Beach Facilities: Well-organized beach amenities, like loungers and umbrellas, are available for beachgoers to enjoy. Greek food, snacks, and beverages are served at many of the beachside cafes and tavernas.

6. Lodging: There are many hotels, flats, and villas in the vicinity of Agios Prokopios Beach, offering lodging alternatives close to the shore. Beautiful views of the Aegean Sea are provided by several of these facilities.

7. Nightlife: There is a vibrant nightlife in Agios Prokopios, with clubs and beach bars providing entertainment till late in the evening. Those wishing to spend the evening by the beach will find a lively scene created by the music, beverages, and waterfront location.

Panoramic views of the surrounding countryside and the Aegean Sea can be enjoyed from the elevated locations surrounding Agios Prokopios Beach. This is a great place to watch the sunset for an unforgettable experience.

9. Convenient Location to Naxos Town: Agios Prokopios is ideally situated near Naxos Town, providing guests with simple access to the island's capital for more facilities, historical landmarks, and cultural events.

10. A welcoming atmosphere for families: Agios Prokopios Beach is suitable for families with its serene seas and well-kept amenities. Children can play safely in the sea because of its gentle entry, and families can make use of the amenities available.

Offering a blend of natural beauty, water sports, facilities, and a vibrant atmosphere that appeals to a varied variety of guests looking for an unforgettable beach experience on Naxos, Agios Prokopios Beach stands out as a well-liked and well-rounded resort.

Plaka

Plaka Beach is a gorgeous length of coastline with long sandy beaches, bright blue waves, and a serene environment. It is situated on the western coast of Naxos, Greece. This is a detailed description of Plaka Beach:

1. Sandy Expanse: Plaka Beach is a popular location for long, leisurely walks along the shoreline, beach activities, and sunbathing due to its broad, smooth, golden sand stretch.

2. Waters That Are Crystal Clear: The beach is well-known for having blue-hued, crystal-clear waves. It is perfect for swimmers because of its mild descent into the sea, and the transparency of the water adds to the whole beach experience.

3. Natural Beauty: Plaka Beach is surrounded by breathtaking scenery, including views of the nearby islands and the Aegean Sea. The beach's beauty is enhanced by the pristine surroundings, which include rolling hills and lush vegetation.

4. Beach Facilities: To ensure that beach goers have a nice day, Plaka Beach offers basic amenities including sunbeds and umbrellas. Greek traditional cuisine and refreshments are served at a number of beachside cafes and tavernas.

5. Water Sports: Although Plaka is renowned for its tranquil surroundings, thrill-seekers can enjoy water sports like paddle boarding and windsurfing. Conditions are generally good, offering a harmonious blend of leisure and entertainment.

6. Tavernas and Beachfront Dining: There are a lot of tavernas and restaurants along the beach where guests may have delectable meals while taking in views of the ocean. Sunset is a particularly popular time to dine on the beach.

7. Family-Friendly Atmosphere: Families with kids can enjoy Plaka Beach because of its gentle slope and peaceful seas. The conveniences and family-friendly setting make it a pleasant place for people of all ages to visit.

8. Sunset Views: Plaka is renowned for its magnificent views of the setting sun. A unique and romantic ambiance is created by the sun sinking over the Aegean Sea and the silhouettes of neighboring islands.

9. Nudist sector: For those looking for a more private and clothes-optional experience, there is a dedicated nudist sector near the southern end of Plaka Beach.

The tranquil environment is as follows: Despite the beach's potential for tourism, particularly in the summer, Plaka manages to preserve its calm and relaxed atmosphere. It's the ideal location for people who want to relax and get away from the busy streets.

For those looking for an unforgettable beach experience in the Greek islands, Plaka Beach on Naxos stands out as a tranquil and attractive location that provides the ideal fusion of natural beauty, recreational activities, and a laid-back environment.

Agia Anna

On the western side of Naxos, Greece, Agia Anna Beach is a well-known coastline strip that is well-known for its gorgeous sandy beaches, glistening waters, and lively environment. This is a detailed description of Agia Anna Beach:

Agia Anna Beach is the perfect place for beach enthusiasts because of its long, sandy beachfront.

1. Sandy beachfront: The beautiful golden sand makes for a cozy environment for leisure activities and sunbathing.

2. Waters That Are Crystal Clear: The seas at the beach are varied shades of blue and are very clear. Swimming is permitted due to the beach's mild slope into the ocean, and the water's clarity adds to the whole beach experience.

3. Water Sports: Agia Anna Beach provides a variety of water sports experiences, such as paddle boarding and windsurfing. Beginners and lovers of water sports will find the area welcoming due to the calm waters and excellent wind conditions.

4. Beach Facilities: Sunbeds and umbrellas are among the many amenities that the beach offers to make tourists comfortable. Additionally, there are cafés and tavernas beside the shore where patrons can partake in local fare and refreshments.

5. Restaurants and Tavernas: Many tavernas and eateries serving fresh seafood, Greek specialties, and refreshing drinks can be found along the shore. A highlight for many guests is dining with a view of the sea and the sound of the waves.

6. Scenic Views: Agia Anna Beach offers breathtaking views of the nearby Paros Island and the Aegean Sea. The expansive views enhance the beach's allure, particularly at dawn and dusk.

7. A welcoming atmosphere for families: Agia Anna Beach is kid-friendly because of the calm seas and the seabed's moderate slope. With a variety of amenities, the family-friendly atmosphere guarantees a good time for all ages.

8. Close to Agia Anna Village: The quaint village of Agia Anna is just next to the beach, making it simple to get to places to stay, eat, and other facilities. The community enhances the seaside destination's allure.

9. Well-liked Tourist Attraction: Agia Anna Beach is one of the island's well-liked tourist attractions, drawing both domestic and foreign visitors. Its appeal is due to the convergence of scenic beauty, outdoor activities, and a vibrant atmosphere.

10. Calm Environment: Even while the beach gets crowded, especially in the summer, it still has a generally tranquil vibe. Guests have the option of exploring the neighboring community, having fun in the water, or relaxing on the beach.

A must-see spot on Naxos, Agia Anna Beach offers the ideal combination of scenic beauty, recreational opportunities, and a lively seaside atmosphere for travelers looking for an unforgettable beach experience in the Greek islands.

Mikri Vigla

Situated on the southwest coast of Naxos, Greece, Mikri Vigla Beach is a charming and varied coastal location that is well-known for its two neighboring beaches, Mikri Vigla North and Mikri Vigla South. This is a detailed description of Mikri Vigla Beach:

1. Two Beaches: - Mikri Vigla Beach is divided into two halves – Mikri Vigla North and Mikri Vigla South. Both provide tourists with unique ambiances and experiences.

2. Vigla North Mikri: Mikri Vigla North is well-known for its golden sandy beach and crystal-clear waters, making it a popular location for swimming and tanning. The beach offers a peaceful setting for relaxation because it is somewhat isolated.

3. Mikri Vigla South: Mikri Vigla South is a popular destination for windsurfers and kitesurfers due to its strong and steady winds. The beach is well-known as one of the top venues for water sports on the island.

4. Windsurfing and Kitesurfing: The windy weather in Mikri Vigla South provides an excellent backdrop for windsurfing and kitesurfing. Both novice and expert surfers may be seen along the beach, and those who want to learn or advance their skills can take advantage of the rental options and schools.

5. Sand Dunes: Sand dunes create a distinctive and picturesque scenery in the vicinity of Mikri Vigla. The beach's natural beauty is enhanced by the dunes, which also present chances for exploration.

6. Beach Facilities: Sunbeds and umbrellas are among the essential beach amenities provided by Mikri Vigla North and South. There might be more amenities at Mikri Vigla South for those who enjoy water sports, like equipment rentals and instruction.

7. Tavernas and cafés: There are beachside cafés and tavernas nearby that provide a variety of regional dishes and cool drinks. Diners can take in the Aegean Sea and the surrounding coastal landscape while dining al fresco.

8. Surrounding Natural Beauty: The sand dunes, the crystal-clear Aegean waves, and the rocky headlands all encircle the beautiful Mikri Vigla Beach. These components work together to provide an eye-catching scene.

9. Sunset Views: Mikri Vigla's west-facing orientation makes it a great spot to catch sunset views. The natural surroundings of the beach coupled with the twilight sky above the Aegean make an enthralling image.

10. Convenience to Naxos Town: Although Mikri Vigla has a somewhat remote feel, it is rather close to Naxos Town, making it simple for guests to access other facilities, historical landmarks, and cultural attractions.

Mikri Vigla Beach is a multipurpose location that provides exciting water sports activities on its southern side and a tranquil atmosphere for relaxing on its northern side. It's a unique place on the island of Naxos because of the way that leisure activities and scenic beauty coexist.

CHAPTER SIX: HISTORICAL SITES

Temple of Apollo

One of the most important religious and cultural hubs of ancient Greece was the Temple of Apollo at Delphi, which is located in central Greece on the foothills of Mount Parnassus. The temple was built in honor of Apollo, the Greek god of archery, music, healing, and prophecy, and dates back to the fourth century BCE.

1. The architectural design:

The temple, with its six columns on the façade and fifteen along the sides, is a prime example of Doric architecture. It was built from local limestone and had a peripheral design, which entails a colonnade encircling the entire building. The sacred omphalos, a representation of the Earth's navel, and the esteemed oracle were kept in the cella, or inner chamber.

2. Delphi Oracle:

The Pythia, a priestess known as the oracle, was the focal point of the Apollo Temple at Delphi. The Pythia was consulted by travelers from all across the ancient world for guidance and prophecies. Ancient Greek politics, the military, and personal choices were influenced by the enigmatic and frequently interpreted predictions of the Oracle.

3. Importance to Culture:

Delphi was revered in ancient Greek religion as the center of the universe. Every four years, contestants from several Greek city-states gathered around the temple for the Pythian Games, an esteemed athletic and musical tournament honoring Apollo.

4. Legends and Mythology:

Greek mythology states that Delphi is the center of the Earth because two eagles that Zeus released met there after taking flight from opposite sides of the planet. The location was also connected to the young Apollo's killing of the terrifying serpent, the Python. The site of the temple was highly significant both symbolically and religiously.

5. Regression and Destroying:

Throughout history, the Temple of Apollo has seen numerous instances of demolition and reconstruction. It was damaged in the Fourth Sacred War in the 4th century BCE, and an earthquake in the 373 BCE completely destroyed it. Although the Romans repaired it, Delphi was ultimately neglected and abandoned as a result of the end of the ancient world.

6. Excavations of Archaeology:

In the 19th and 20th centuries, the site was the subject of major archaeological excavations that not only revealed the temple but also other buildings and artifacts that shed light on the daily lives and religious rituals of the ancient Greeks.

As a UNESCO World Heritage Site, the Temple of Apollo at Delphi draws tourists with its historical significance and the ruins of an old sanctuary that was once vital to the political and spiritual life of the classical world.

Kouros of Melanes

The term "kouroi" refers to a group of ancient Greek sculptures that are housed in the village of Melanes on the Greek island of Naxos. The term "kouros" refers to free-standing Greek statues depicting young men in the nude who are usually gods or heroes. The incomplete state and fascinating history of the Kouros of Melanes make it unique.

1. Place:On the island of Naxos, in the village of Melanes, there is an outdoor sanctuary where one can find the Kouros statues. There are further historic relics and ruins at the location.

2. The quantity of statues: In Melanes, there are three noteworthy Kouros statues. The largest and most well-known is known as the

Melanes Kouros. It is thought that the two smaller ones are connected to the larger Kouros.

3. Melanese Couros: The main statue, sometimes referred to as the Great Kouros of Melanes, is approximately 6.4 meters (21 feet) tall. It is said to have been carved in the seventh century BCE out of Naxian marble. Remarkably, the sculptors left this Kouros partially completed, meaning it is still unfinished.

4. Underdeveloped State: The Kouros of Melanes is exceptional because it offers a unique window into the making of ancient sculpture. Its fragmentary state may have been caused by a variety of factors, including changing artistic tastes, budgetary limitations, or the death of the sculptors.

5. Technical Specifications: The Kouros sculptures have the stiff frontal attitude, rigorous symmetry, and the Egyptian-inspired stance with one foot advanced that are hallmarks of Archaic Greek sculpture. Given the Greek emphasis on the perfect human form, the figures are depicted in their undies.

6. Traditions and Worship in the Area: The Kouros statues were probably made in a nearby workshop with a particular religious or burial function in mind. Kouroui were frequently offered as votive offerings at sanctuaries or on tomb markers in ancient Greece.

7. Importance for Archaeology: The finding of the Kouros statues in Melanes advances knowledge of Greek artistic traditions and sculptural methods. The major Kouros' incomplete state sheds light on the methodical manner in which gigantic sculptures were produced in the Archaic era.

8. Preservation & Conservation: The Kouros statues at Melanes have been the subject of preservation and protection efforts. Even though these priceless relics have weathered over the ages due to exposure to the elements, conservation efforts are still being made to safeguard their longevity.

The Kouros of Melanes stands as a stunning witness to the craftsmanship and artistic techniques of ancient Greece, affording a unique and unfinished peek into the realm of Archaic sculpture. These amazing statues are visible to visitors to Melanes in the exact location where they were made, surrounded by the island of Naxos' rich cultural heritage.

Bazeos Tower

Bazeos Tower in Sangri is one of the most recognizable sites in Naxos, located on the main route that connects the Chora with the highland villages of Halki and Filoti. The tower was erected in this exact spot in the seventeenth century to protect the locals from the regular pirate invasions.

Bazeos Tower was once the Timios Stavros (True Cross) monastery, but during the 19th century it was progressively abandoned.

Subsequently, the tower came into the possession of the Bazeos family, who used it as their vacation home until the last descendent made the decision to renovate it so that it could accommodate cultural events.

Since 2001, the famous Naxos Festival at Bazeos Tower has been held every summer. It features events of cultural significance together with modern art.

CHAPTER SEVEN: ACTIVITIES AND ADVENTURE

Hiking Trails

The largest island in Greece's Cyclades, Naxos, is a great place for hikers because of its beautiful and varied environment. There are numerous routes on the island that pass through traditional villages, mountains, valleys, and coastal regions. Below is a summary of some of the most notable hiking routes in Naxos:

1. **Mount Zeus (Zas):**
   - **Description:** The tallest point in the Cyclades is Mount Zeus, also referred to as Mount Zas. The starting point of the summit trail is close to Filoti settlement.

Beautiful vistas of the island and the Aegean Sea may be seen from the summit.
- Difficulty: Moderate to strenuous, particularly in the ascending regions.

2. **Koronos Trail - Apiranthos:**
- Description: This trail links the two quaint towns of Koronos and Apiranthos. It gives views of Naxian architecture and travels along traditional stone-paved routes through verdant surroundings.
- Difficulty:** Moderate.

3. **Melanes - Kouros of Apollonas Trail:**
- Description: This trail begins in Melanes village and ends close to the incomplete Kouros statue. It offers both scenic natural beauty and fascinating archaeological features.
- Level of difficulty:** Moderately easy.

4. **Halki - Tragea Valley Trail:**
    - Description: This trail starts in Halki village and goes through the Tragea Valley, which is renowned for its traditional citrus orchards and olive groves. A stroll across the Naxian countryside is nice.
    - Difficulty:** Simple.
5. **Aliko - Coastal Walk at Glyfada Beach:**
    - Description: This coastal walk leads you from Aliko Beach to Glyfada Beach, going through sandy coasts, sand dunes, and cedar forests. It's a terrific alternative for individuals who prefer a mix of beach and wildlife.
    - Difficulty:** Simple.
6. **Eggares Olive Grove Trail - Kaloxylos:**

- Description: The olive groves close to Eggares and Kaloxylos villages are explored by this trail. Naxos's agricultural past is revealed on this stroll, which is peaceful and in the aroma of olive trees.
- Difficulty:** Simple.

7. *Agios Prokopios - Agia Anna Coastal Path:
- Description: Take a stroll along the picturesque seashore along the path that runs between Agia Anna and Agios Prokopios. This walk is especially fun around sunset and offers breathtaking views of the Aegean Sea.
- Difficulty:** Simple.

It is important to investigate local circumstances, get accurate maps, and, if needed, employ a local guide before starting any trekking expedition in Naxos. Additionally, especially in the warmer months, remember to include necessities like water, appropriate footwear, and sun protection. Hiking fans will find Naxos to be a worthwhile vacation because of the island's varied routes, which accommodate varying fitness levels and interests.

Windsurfing and Kiteboarding

Naxos is a well-liked location for kiteboarding and windsurfing aficionados due to its stunning beaches and ideal wind conditions. It's the perfect place to enjoy these water activities, with a variety of sites for both novice and expert riders on the island. An extensive guide on windsurfing and kiteboarding in Naxos is provided here:

Surfing the wind in Naxos:

- Beach Agios Georgios: One of the island's primary windsurfing hotspots is Agios Georgios. The beach has a considerable amount of sandy shoreline and is well-known for its consistent summertime Meltemi breezes.
- Restrictions: Windsurfing is made easier by the Meltemi wind, which usually blows from the north. From novice to expert riders, the bay is appropriate for all ability levels.

- The Beach at Laguna:Laguna Beach, which is close to the town of Naxos, is

another well-liked windsurfing location. It's ideal for learning and skill improvement because of the shallow waters and steady winds.
- Restrictions:* Windsurfers can enjoy a steady environment thanks to the small lagoon and the Meltemi breeze. On the beach, there are options for lessons and equipment rentals.

- Mikri Vigla Beach: Famed for its lengthy sandy shore, Mikri Vigla is separated into two sections: one for kitesurfing and one for windsurfing. The windsurfing area provides fantastic conditions and a lively environment.
- Restrictions: Windsurfing is consistently possible due to the dominance of the Meltemi breeze. All skill levels can use

the bay, and there are rental shops with equipment and instruction available.

Naxos is a great place to ski

- Mikri Vigla Beach (Kitesurfing Side): One of the most popular places to kiteboard in Naxos is the kitesurfing side of Mikri Vigla. It provides a sizable sand beach with ideal wind conditions.
- Restrictions: Kiteboarders have the perfect conditions thanks to the Meltemi breeze and the wide beach. For all skill levels, there are rental shops and kite courses.

- **Alyko Beach:** Kiteboarders are becoming more and more accustomed to Alyko Beach because of its steady winds and clean waters. It's a more private location

than others, offering a peaceful kitesurfing experience.
- Restrictions: Kiteboarders seeking a more tranquil setting will find Alyko Beach appealing due to its uncrowded character and the reliable Meltemi breeze.

- Plaka Beach: Plaka is a lengthy, gorgeous beach that draws visitors who want to kiteboard and windsurf. Particularly in the Meltemi season, it provides a roomy place for kiteboarding.
- Restrictions: Kiteboarding is made reliable by the Meltemi wind, and there's plenty of beach area for launches and rides.

Naxos has several choices for windsurfing and kiteboarding, whether you're a novice looking for instruction or an expert rider seeking difficult conditions. For an exhilarating and pleasurable experience on the water, it is advised to verify local wind conditions, consult with knowledgeable instructors, and make sure safety precautions are taken.

Scuba Diving

With its pristine seas and abundant marine life, Naxos is becoming a more and more popular destination for scuba divers of all skill levels, from novices to experts, the island has a variety of dive locations. An extensive guide on scuba diving in Naxos is provided here:

Dive Locations:

- Koufonissi Island:Koufonissi Island, southeast of Naxos, has fascinating underwater scenery. Divers can

investigate marine life, walls, and sea caves.
- Features: Schools of fish, vibrant sponges, and underwater arches make Koufonissi a well-liked diving spot.

- Papa's Reef:Located close to Agia Anna, Papa's Reef is renowned for its intriguing terrain, which includes rocks, cliffs, and fissures, as well as its abundant marine fauna.
- Features: Divers may come across different fish species, moray eels, and octopuses. Both skilled and novice divers can enjoy this spot.

- The Parthenos Tragedy: An artificial reef formed by a sunken cargo ship is called the Parthenos Wreck. It is located

off the coast of Naxos and is a popular wreck diving destination.
- Features: Numerous marine species, such as groupers and schools of lesser fish, can be found living on the wreck.

- island of Dragonisiis situated southwest of Naxos and features intriguing rock formations, walls, and underwater caverns.
- Features: Divers can explore sea caverns and come across nudibranchs, groupers, and barracudas, among other marine species.

Dive Centers:

1. Blue Fin Divers Naxos: For both novice and expert divers, this Agia Anna diving center provides a variety of courses. They plan boat dives to different locations near Naxos.

2. Scuba Diving Center Naxos: This dive center, which is located in Agios Prokopios, offers guided dives and PADI training. They prioritize environmental consciousness and safety while serving divers of all skill levels.

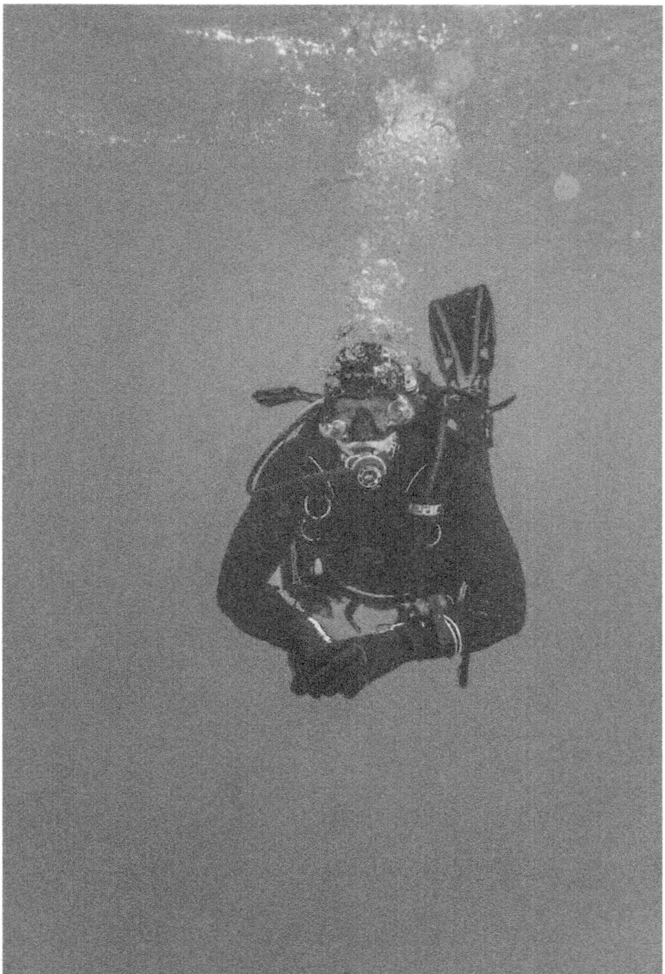

CHAPTER EIGHT: LOCAL CUISINE

Traditional Naxian Dishes

Because it is an agriculturally wealthy and fertile island in the Cyclades, Naxos has a rich culinary legacy that is based on regional products and customs. The following is a detailed list of some of the typical Naxian foods you may come across:

1. Patates Lemonates (Citron Sauced Potatoes): This is a zesty and savory side dish made with Naxian potatoes sautéed in a lemon-based sauce. The island is well known for its superior potatoes.

2. Arseniko Naxou: A typical Naxian cheese prepared from a blend of goat and sheep milk is called arseniko. It tastes very different and is usually eaten grated or sliced on different foods.

3. Citrus Liqueur: A distinctive liqueur called Kitron is created from the leaves of the citron tree. It is frequently consumed as an aperitif or in cocktails because of its zesty flavor. The settlement of Halki is the hub of the kitron producing process.

4. Tomate with Lamb (Arni Sto Fourno): In Naxos, lamb is a favorite dish. Arni Sto Fourno is a slow-cooked lamb dish that includes potatoes, garlic, and local herbs. Meat that is delicious and soft is the outcome.

5. Cheese with Graviera from Naxian: Made from cow's milk, graviera is a hard cheese. With its distinct flavor character, Naxian Graviera is frequently grated over food or offered as a component of cheese platters.

6. Zambonopitta: A classic sweet pie filled with cheese, sugar, and eggs from the area is called zambonopitta. It is frequently consumed at festivals and celebrations because of its rich, decadent flavor.

7. Details: Loukoumades are honey-drizzled dough balls that resemble doughnuts, dusted with sesame seeds or cinnamon, and deep-fried. In Naxos, they're a well-liked confection.

8. Marathopita: A savory pie made with onions, fennel, and other local herbs is called marathopita. These components work together to give the pie a unique flavor.

9. Tomatokeftede: Tomatokeftedes are cooked with seasonal tomatoes, herbs, and occasionally feta cheese. They showcase the fresh food of the island and make a delicious appetizer or snack.

10. Revithada, or Chickpea Soup: Cooked in clay pots, revithada is a substantial soup made with chickpeas. Chickpeas, olive oil, onions, and herbs are combined to create a tasty and nourishing dish.

11. Tsatsiki Naxou: The addition of Naxian cheeses to this traditional Greek tsatsiki makes for a rich, savory dip or sauce.

12. Algae: Seafood dishes are popular in Naxos because of its coastal environment. Fresh seafood, including octopus and fish, are cooked in a variety of ways, most frequently by grilling or stewing it with olive oil and local herbs.

Discovering the island's rich culinary legacy while on Naxos can be achieved by visiting neighborhood restaurants and traditional tavernas. The distinctive and mouth watering flavors of Naxian cuisine are enhanced by the use of fresh, locally obtained ingredients.

Popular Restaurants

1. Chora (Axiotissa): At Naxos Town (Chora), Axiotissa is well-known for its traditional Greek cuisine made with organic, locally sourced ingredients. It's a favorite among both locals and tourists because of the warm ambiance and traditional cuisines.

2. Chora (Scirocco): In Naxos Town, Scirocco is a seafood-focused eatery situated in a lovely coastal location. Freshly caught seafood, grilled octopus, and other Mediterranean delicacies are among the menu's many offerings.

3. O Giorgis, the Chora: O Giorgis, a restaurant known for its Greek and Mediterranean food, is located in Naxos Town's Old Market district. The restaurant's menu features grilled foods and regional specialties, and its patio creates a lovely atmosphere.

4. Agios Prokopios (Meze2): Meze2, which is close to the well-liked Agios Prokopios Beach, serves a selection of mezes, or appetizers, and authentic Greek cuisine. The eatery is well-known for its outside dining and welcoming ambiance.

5. Chora (Scalco): Located in the center of Naxos Town, Scalco is a contemporary eatery offering a wide selection of dishes. It offers a variety of options for varying tastes by fusing classic Greek flavors with modern twists.

6. To Elliniko (Chora): A family-run taverna called To Elliniko is situated in Naxos Town's Old Market and is well-known for its friendly service and authentic Greek cuisine. A selection of grilled meats, fresh salads, and regional delicacies are offered on the menu.

7. Petrino (Chora): Nestled in a picturesque courtyard in Naxos Town, Petrino serves a menu that highlights regional delicacies. It is especially well-known for its inventive salads, vegetarian selections, and Greek wine list.

8. Agia Anna, or Katsourbos: Greek classics and seafood are the specialties of Agia Anna's beachside eatery Katsourbos. Beautiful views of the Aegean Sea are provided by the setting, which makes for a tranquil dining experience.

9. O Vasilis (Plaka): Plaka's O Vasilis is a waterfront taverna well-known for its fresh seafood and authentic Greek fare. The ability to eat on the beach and the relaxed ambiance are frequently appreciated by visitors.

10. Apostolis (Agios Prokopios): Apostolis is a Greek and Mediterranean-style taverna located close to Agios Prokopios Beach. It is well-known for its hearty servings, welcoming staff, and menu that accommodates a wide range of tastes.

11. Agios Georgios Beach (Naxian): As its name implies, Naxian on the Beach is a fine-dining establishment situated directly on Agios Georgios Beach. It emphasizes local, fresh ingredients while serving a blend of Greek and foreign cuisine.

When visiting Naxos, try to go out of the main towns and find quaint little tavernas and family-run businesses that add to the island's diverse culinary offerings. Remember that restaurant acclaim can change with the seasons, and it's usually a good idea to ask around for recommendations for the best places to eat right now.

Food Festivals

Like many other Greek islands, Naxos celebrates the rich culinary legacy of the area with a number of food festivals held throughout the year. Keep in mind that precise festival dates may vary from year to year, so it's advisable to check local calendars for the most accurate information. Below is a detailed list of some of the most important cuisine events in Naxos:

1. Festival ton Kitron, Citron Festival: The Citron Festival, which takes place in the village of Halki, honors the unusual citrus fruit known as kitron, which is used to produce the well-known Naxian liquor. Usually, the festival has music, cultural activities, and tastings.

2. Festival of Potatoes (Patatokeftedes): The Potato Festival, which is frequently held in the village of Mesi, honors the quality potatoes that

Naxos is known for. In addition to other regional specialties, guests can savor potato-based foods such patatokeftedes (potato fritters).

3. Dionysia Festival (Dionysia Naxou): Naxos Town (Chora) hosts the Dionysia Festival, which honors regional goods like cheese, wine, and cuisine. Live music, cultural activities, and the chance to try Naxian food are frequently included.

4. The Saki Festival (Rakitzia): This event honors the grape-based beverage known as raki, a classic Greek alcohol. Attendees can sample several variations of this drink. Local cuisine, live music, and a joyous environment are frequently featured during the event.

5.The Fisherman's Feast, also known as Giorti ton Psarion: The Fisherman's Feast honors the island's maritime history and is held in fishing villages like Agia Anna. Local fishermen produce a variety of fresh seafood delicacies that visitors can enjoy.

6. Giorti ton Aligarion (Aligaria Festival): This event in the village of Filoti honors the traditional dish known as "," which is cooked from goat or lamb liver. There is usually traditional music and dance throughout the celebration.

7. Giorti tou Krasiou Wine: The wine industry on Naxos is expanding, and the Wine Festival offers a chance to sample regional wines, discover winemaking techniques, and savor food pairings. It frequently happens in different parts of the island.

8. Paschalina's Easter Celebrations: Easter is a big deal on Naxos, and traditional Easter feasts are a big element of the celebrations, however it's not just a food festival. During this time, roasted lamb, tsoureki (Easter bread), and other delights are savored.

9. Giorti ton Elion Olive Festival: Olive growing has a long history in Naxos, as it does on many other Greek islands. The Olive Festival honors this legacy by hosting events centered around olive oil, tastings, and traditional recipes that use olives.

10. Giorti ton Kerasion Cherry Festival: The cherry harvest is celebrated in the village of Keramoti with the Cherry Festival. Fresh cherries, goods made with cherries, and a variety of delectable dishes made with this seasonal fruit are available to visitors.

Taking part in these culinary celebrations offers a singular chance to interact with Naxian customs, sample regional cuisine, and bask in the kind hospitality of the island. For the most current details on festival dates and events, don't forget to consult your local event calendars.

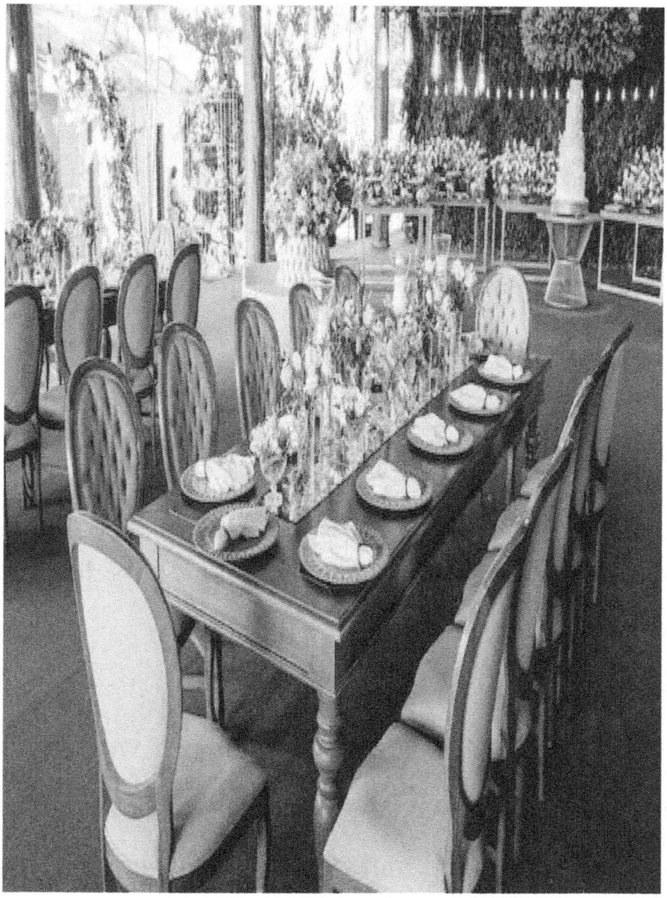

CHAPTER NINE :NIGHTLIFE AND ENTERTAINMENT

Bars and Clubs

The stunning Greek island of Naxos, located in the Aegean Sea, has a thriving nightlife culture with a wide range of pubs and clubs to suit various preferences.

Bars:

1. Bar Papagalos: Papagalos Bar is a well-liked location in Naxos Town that is well-known for its laid-back vibe and delectable beverages. It's a great location to relax with nice staff and outdoor seating.

2. Drop Bar: Situated in Naxos Town, this hip bar is well-known for its elaborate drink menu

and distinctive décor. Swing Bar offers a wide selection of inventive and traditional cocktails to suit every taste.

3. Bar Babylonia: Located in the center of Naxos Town, Babylonia Bar is well-known for its vibrant and lively live music events. It's a popular choice for both residents and visitors.

clubs:

1. The Escape Club: Escape Club in Agios Prokopios is the place to go if you enjoy electronic music and a bustling dance floor. The club is a popular destination for anyone looking for an unforgettable night out because it features both local and foreign DJs.

2. The Ocean Club: Ocean Club, which is tucked away by the shore in Agia Anna, combines live music, seaside views, and a fun atmosphere. The club regularly throws themed

gatherings and events, guaranteeing a wide range of entertainment options.

3. The Gazzaki Club: Gazaki Club, which is situated in Naxos Town, is a well-liked option for people who like a blend of Greek and mainstream music. For a night of dancing and mingling, it's a great choice because of its lively atmosphere and friendly audience.

Naxos offers a vibrant nightlife scene that accommodates a variety of tastes, whether you prefer the quiet atmosphere of a tavern or the throbbing sounds of a club. Remember that the island's nightlife peaks in the summer when visitors swarm to take advantage of the pleasant weather and lively environment.

Cultural Events

Due to its long history and rich cultural legacy, Naxos is a popular destination for both tourists and locals. Throughout the year, the city stages a range of cultural events. These celebrations honor the island's customs, artistic expression, and distinct culture.

1. Festival Naxos: The Naxos Festival, which takes place every year in the summer, offers a wide variety of cultural events, such as dance performances, music concerts, theater productions, and art exhibitions. The festival frequently makes use of Naxos' historical landmarks, holding events in famous locations like the Portara, an antiquated marble gate with a view of the ocean.

2. Bazeos Tower's Naxos Festival: This cultural program showcases the creative side of the island and is held at the Bazeos Tower. In the stunning environment of the tower and its surroundings, guests can take in dance

performances, art exhibitions, and concerts of classical music.

3. Events Celebrating Folklore: Naxos is proud of its rich traditions in folklore, which are honored through a number of events. Events including music festivals, traditional dance performances, and cultural get-togethers shed light on the island's past.

4. Religious Festivals: The cultural calendar of Naxos heavily emphasizes religious festivals. Religious ceremonies, processions, and traditional festivities unite locals and visitors during celebrations like the Feast of Panagia, which honors the Assumption of the Virgin Mary.

5. Events at the Venetian Castle: Several cultural events take place against the backdrop of the Venetian Castle in Naxos Town. The old castle walls are frequently the site of concerts,

plays, and art exhibits, providing a distinctive fusion of history and culture.

6. Agricultural and Food Festivals: Celebrations such as the Naxos Potato Festival honor the region's agricultural heritage. These events offer a flavor of the island's culinary culture by showcasing regional produce, traditional recipes, and gourmet delights.

7. Carnival Festivities: In Naxos, the Carnival season is marked by vibrant parades, vibrant costumes, and joyous celebrations. It's a time when locals and tourists gather to celebrate the festive atmosphere, which is further enhanced by traditional dance and music performances.

In addition to giving one a better understanding of the history and customs of Naxos, going to these cultural events also gives one a chance to interact with the locals and take in the lively cultural environment of the island. Remember that event dates might change, so when making travel plans, it's best to check local calendars and tourism websites for the most recent details.

Folklore Evenings

Indulge in the rich cultural legacy of the island during a Folklore Evening in Naxos, an enthralling event. These gatherings usually feature traditional dance, music, and rituals, offering an unforgettable cultural experience and a window into Naxian folklore.

1. Traditional Music: Live performances of traditional Naxian music are a common element of folklore evenings. Local instruments like the bouzouki and lyre are played by musicians, who fill the air with songs that have been passed down through the generations.

2. Traditional Dance Performances: Folk dance is a highlight of these evenings, with local dance ensembles showcasing traditional Naxian dances. These dances, which incorporate motions inspired by daily life, harvest festivals, and more, frequently represent the island's agricultural history.

3. Attire and Costumes: Participants and performers frequently dress in traditional attire that highlights the island's diversity of cultures. These costumes, which depict many Naxos locations and historical eras, are embellished with vivid colors, elaborate patterns, and symbolic motifs.

4. Folktales and Storytelling: Storytelling events during folklore evenings often feature villagers reciting customary stories, tales, and folklore. These stories frequently provide light on

historical events that occurred on the island as well as Naxian superstitions and beliefs.

5. Culinary Treasures: A gastronomic component may be added to folklore evenings to improve the entire experience. Savoring traditional Naxian cuisine enables visitors to partake in the culinary customs of the island.

6. Audience Involvement: Numerous folklore events promote audience involvement by encouraging guests to partake in the festivities and dances. This interactive feature helps communities and visitors feel more connected to one another.

7. Location and Ambience: Traditional tavernas, outdoor spaces, or historical sites are common venues for folklore evenings. The encounter is enhanced by the allure of Naxos's natural beauty and the quaint environment.

8. Occasion-Based Festivities: Folklore evenings may coincide with particular religious holidays or seasonal celebrations, depending on the time of year. Events held during the Carnival season, for instance, may have lively themes and outfits.

Taking part in a Folklore Evening in Naxos offers the chance to experience the island's genuineness and establish a connection with its hospitable and friendly locals, in addition to being a cultural adventure. If visitors are looking for a more in-depth experience with Naxian traditions and customs, they might check with their hotels or local tourist offices about scheduled folklore events.

CHAPTER TEN: SHOPPING

Local Markets

For tourists interested in discovering the island's genuine flavors, fresh food, handcrafted crafts, and traditional goods, the local markets of Naxos provide a fascinating experience. Here's a detailed rundown:

1. Naxos Town Market: Naxos Town, or Chora, has a thriving market where visitors and locals alike may find a wide range of products. With countless vendors offering fruits, vegetables, cheeses, olives, herbs, and other regional goods, the market is a hive of activity.

- Agricultural Products: The market features a wide range of fruits and vegetables, honey, locally produced olive oil, and the famous Naxian potatoes, among other agricultural products from the island. Taste and buy these fresh, organic products are available to visitors.

- Dairy and Cheese: Naxos is well-known for its cheese, especially arseniko and graviera. Samples and purchases of these delicious cheeses, which are frequently made by regional farmers and artisans, are available at the market.

- Seafood Market: Because of its seaside location, Naxos has a bustling seafood market where tourists may purchase a variety of seafood, including freshly caught fish. Both diners and restaurants come to this area of the market to purchase the catch of the day.

- Handcrafted Items: In addition to culinary items, handcrafted goods may be found in abundance at the market. Handcrafted goods such as jewelry, woven fabrics, ceramics, and traditional Naxian souvenirs are exhibited by the local artists. It's a great spot to find souvenirs and unusual gifts.
- 6. Traditional delicacies: The vendors selling traditional Naxian delicacies will appeal to sweet tooths. From cookies and nougats to honey-soaked pastries like baklava, the market offers a chance to savor the island's delicious sweets.
- 7. Local Wines: The market in Naxos frequently contains stands or stores selling wines from the region. Naxos has a developing wine industry. A sense of the island's viticulture can be added to

visitors' experiences by tasting and buying wines made from native grape varietals.

- 8. Events related to culture and flea markets: Events related to culture and flea markets are occasionally held in Naxos Town. These gatherings bring together a wider variety of vendors, providing unique products, antiques, and vintage things in addition to the usual market fare.
- Context of the Market: When the stalls are completely filled in the morning, the market ambiance is extremely bright and lively. An immersive and genuine experience is created by the aromas of fresh vegetables, the sounds of sellers calling out their wares, and the vibrant displays.

Discovering the local markets in Naxos is an immersive experience that delves into the essence of the island's culinary and cultural customs, extending beyond a mere shopping trip. The markets in Naxos offer a fascinating tapestry of local life, whether you're looking for fresh produce for a picnic or mementos to commemorate your stay.

Souvenirs

Naxos offers a broad assortment of souvenirs, allowing tourists to take home a bit of the island's culture, workmanship, and natural beauty. This is a detailed list of all the mementos that you could locate in Naxos:

1. Pottery and Ceramics: Naxos has a strong tradition of pottery manufacture. Popular mementos are handcrafted ceramic dishes,

bowls, and decorative pieces. The traditional patterns and motifs found in the designs are frequently influenced by the history of the island.

2. Olive Wood Products: The island is home to many olive trees, and from their wood, artists create beautiful objects. Gifts for visitors include cutting boards, cutlery, and other items crafted from this indigenous wood.

3. Woven fabrics: Skilled weavers in the area create elaborate fabrics such as tablecloths, scarves, and rugs. These objects frequently have traditional hues and designs that pay homage to Naxos' rich cultural past.

4. Jewelry:Naxian craftsmen craft exquisite items that draw inspiration from the island's scenic surroundings. Seek for jewelry embellished with evil-eye motifs or patterns

derived from the local flora and wildlife. Two metals that are often utilized are silver and gold.

5. Local Products and Honey: Naxos is renowned for its premium honey, which guests can purchase in jars to take home. Beeswax candles and skincare products, among other honey-based products, are also well-liked mementos.

6. Cheese from Naxian: Considering the island's stellar cheese reputation, bringing some regional cheeses like arseniko or graviera home makes for a scrumptious and distinctive memento. Choose solutions that come packaged and are convenient to transport.

7. Customary Sweets: Satisfy your sweet craving with customary Naxian sweets such as almond sweets, pasteli (bars with sesame seeds and honey), or baklava. These sweets make

delicious gifts and are frequently elegantly packed.

8. Local Wines: Naxos is home to a burgeoning wine industry. Bringing a bottle home is a great way to bring a little piece of the island with you. Select from wines produced using native grape types.

9. Crafts Inspired by Seashells and the Seaside: Naxos's breathtaking beaches serve as an inspiration for crafts made of seashells and other coastal materials. Look for jewelry made of seashells, décor pieces, or paintings with seaside views.

10. Iconic Symbols: Memorabilia with significant and unique symbols, such the Temple of Apollo's labyrinth design or Portara (Apollo's Gate), can be found.

11. Hand-painted Ceramics: View hand-painted ceramics with scenes from Naxian life or with classic Greek patterns. Bright colors and complex designs are frequently used to adorn plates, mugs, and decorative tiles.

Naxos has a broad selection of mementos that encapsulate the spirit of this charming Greek island, whether you're looking for gastronomic treats, creative works of art, or useful everyday products. When selecting your keepsakes, think about patronizing regional companies and artists to guarantee a genuine and sentimental keepsake of your visit to Naxos.

Art and Handicrafts

With its extensive cultural legacy, Naxos is a veritable gold mine for lovers of fine art and handicrafts. The island is renowned for its talented craftspeople who create a wide range of handcrafted goods, each of which captures the distinct essence of Naxos. This is a thorough guide explaining what to look for and how to buy art and handicrafts in Naxos:

1. Pottery & Ceramics: There is a long history of pottery in Naxos, and the region's craftspeople produce both decorative and useful ceramics. See the pottery being made by visiting the studios in Naxos Town and nearby villages such as Damalas. Bright colors and classic Greek motifs are common in these pieces.

2. Textiles and Weaving: The island's talented weavers create elaborate textiles such as tablecloths, clothes, and rugs. Visit the traditional weavers' workshops in the villages of Filoti and Chalki. Traditional designs are

frequently included into handwoven textiles, lending a hint of Naxian culture.

3. Creations from Olive Wood: Olive wood is crafted by artists in Naxos, a region known for its profusion of olive plants. Look for chopping boards, cutlery, and accent pieces in gift shops, local markets, or straight out of village workshops.

4. Jewelry: Naxos features outstanding jewelers who produce unique pieces inspired by the island's history and natural beauty. Customary emblems such as the evil eye are frequently applied to designs. Visit artisan studios in the villages or peruse jewelry stores in Naxos Town.

5. Art galleries and paintings: Naxos Town is home to several art galleries that display sculptures, paintings, and modern pieces created by Greek and local artists. There are many

galleries in the Castle neighborhood, with a wide variety of styles to choose from. To purchase one-of-a-kind items, check out the exhibitions or attend gallery openings.

6. Seashell and Beach-Inspired Crafts: Craftspeople in coastal regions make seashell jewelry, beach-inspired décor, and artwork, among other crafts. These distinctive and endearing designs are frequently found at beachside stores and booths.

7. Customized Appearances: A few craftspeople specialize in creating customary Naxian attire. Even while they might not be appropriate for daily wear, these are interesting and genuine works of art. To understand more about the workmanship required, visit nearby costume workshops.

8. Artistic pottery: Hand-painted pottery portraying traditional Greek motifs or scenes

from Naxian life are common. The ceramicists in the area use complex designs and vivid colors in their works. These are available at marketplaces, souvenir shops, and ceramic studios.

9. Wood sculptures: Naxos artisans create detailed wood sculptures that frequently include mythological characters, animals, or conventional themes. Explore workshops or artisan markets to find these intricate and creative works of art.

10. Handmade Soaps and Skincare Items: A few local craftspeople specialize in creating skincare items with natural components. Specialty stores carry handmade soaps, lotions, and essential oils derived from local botanicals.

To acquire these unique art and handicrafts in Naxos, explore local markets, souvenir shops, and artist studios. Talk to the artists whenever you can to find out about the processes and sources of inspiration for their works. Additionally, attending cultural events and festivals may provide opportunities to acquire handmade things directly from artists. Supporting regional artisans while selecting mementos will provide a genuine and significant link to Naxos' cultural history.

CHAPTER ELEVEN: DAY TRIPS

Small Cyclades

The Small Cyclades, a group of lovely islands located near Naxos in the Aegean Sea, offer a superb chance for a day trip from Naxos. This is a thorough guide on traveling around the Small Cyclades:

1. Islands in the Small Cyclades: Iraklia, Schinoussa, Donoussa, and Koufonisia are islands in the Small Cyclades. Every island has its own distinct charm, complete with immaculate beaches, glistening oceans, and a laid-back vibe. Due to their close proximity, day visits to the Small Cyclades usually include visiting one or two islands.

2. Day Trip Options: Koufonisia combined with either Schinoussa or Iraklia is a common combination.

3. Koufonisia: The most popular and frequently traveled island in the Small Cyclades is Koufonisia. Ano Koufonisi and Kato Koufonisi are its two main components. Discover stunning beaches such as Finikas, Italida, and Pori. Explore the quaint village of Chora, which features typical Cycladic architecture and quaint alleyways.

4. Antalia: Iraklia is renowned for its peace and scenic surroundings. Nature enthusiasts will appreciate this place because of the hiking trails that lead to private beaches and overlooks. Popular places to explore are Livadi and the beach at Agios Georgios.

5. Schinoussa: With a relaxed vibe, Schinoussa is a smaller, less developed island. Explore the

main village, Chora, with its white-washed buildings, and sandy beaches like Tsigouri and Livadi.

6. Donoussa: The least crowded island in the Small Cyclades, Donoussa is ideal for a peaceful getaway. Admire the beaches in Kedros and Livadi and stroll around Stavros, the largest village.

7. Ferry Connections: Day trip planning is made simple by the ferry that connects Naxos to the Small Cyclades. It's best to check the timetables ahead of time as the ferry schedules sometimes change.

8. scheduled Tours: Travel agencies in Naxos offer scheduled day trips to the Small Cyclades. Ferry transfers, guided tours, and free time for personal exploration are frequently included in these itineraries.

Activities: In the Small Cyclades, visitors can go hiking, swimming, and dine at tavernas by the sea to sample traditional food. Visitors can select an island according to their interests as each one offers a unique experience.

Utilitarian Advice: Bring necessities for exploration, such as water, sunscreen, and cozy shoes. Be mindful of ferry timetables to ensure a smooth return to Naxos.

A day trip from Naxos to the Small Cyclades offers a peek of these islands' pristine splendor. Whether you prefer the bustling ambiance of Koufonisia or the quiet landscapes of Iraklia, each island in the Small Cyclades offers a distinct and memorable experience for a day excursion from Naxos.

Apollonas Village

Situated on Naxos' northern coast, Apollonas Village is a quaint spot that makes a great day excursion from the main town. This is a thorough guide to discovering Apollonas:

Getting There: Apollonas is approximately a one-hour drive from Naxos Town. You can ride a local bus, rent a car, or hail a cab. The drive along the shore is picturesque and offers amazing vistas.

Kouros Archaeological Site: A prominent feature of Apollonas is the enormous incomplete statue known as Kouros, which dates to the 6th century BC. The Kouros offers insights into Greek sculpture and is located in an outdoor archeological site.

Beaches: Apollonas is a great place for swimming and tanning because of its gorgeous beaches. With its calm ambiance and crystal-clear waves, the main beach provides a soothing setting for a seaside break.

Restaurants and Tavernas: Apollonas offers a variety of classic eateries where you may enjoy regional Naxian food. Highlights of dining in this quaint community include fresh seafood, locally produced products, and traditional dishes.

Village Square and Coffee Shops: Discover the village square's charming little stores, cafés, and medieval architecture. It's a nice spot to take in the relaxed atmosphere and sip on a Greek coffee or something refreshing.

Exploration and Hiking: Apollonas is a great place for hikers because it is surrounded by beautiful scenery. There are several paths that lead to vantage places where you can take in the northern region of Naxos' breathtaking scenery.

Cultural and Folk Events: Check for any cultural or folk events happening in Apollonas during your visit. Occasionally, the hamlet holds festivals or shows, offering a special chance to take in the customs and entertainment of the area.

Photograph Possibilities: Apollonas provides scenic vistas and photogenic scenery. Photography enthusiasts will find this combination of the Kouros, the sea, and the old architecture to be quite intriguing.

Products from the Area: Look through neighborhood stores to discover Naxian goods, souvenirs, and handcrafted items. Look for products like wines, olive oil, or locally produced traditional sweets.

Byzantine Church of Panagia Phaneromeni: Go to the Panagia Phaneromeni Byzantine Church, which is situated in Apollonas. This historical site highlights the island's rich legacy and gives your visit a cultural and religious element.

Utilitarian Advice: If you intend to hike about the hamlet, wear comfortable shoes for exploration. Since Naxos' northern region might receive intense sunlight, remember to include a hat, water bottle, and sunscreen.

Apollonas Village provides a beautiful combination of environment, history, and traditional Greek village life for a day trip. Apollonas offers a tranquil and enthralling respite from the busy Naxos Town, whether your interests lie in archaeology, beach relaxing, or sampling local food.

Filoti Village

Located in the center of Naxos, Filoti Village is a picturesque and historically significant site that is perfect for a day trip. This is a thorough guide for traveling around Filoti:

Getting There: Filoti can be reached by car from Naxos Town in about 20 minutes. Easy access is made possible by taxis, rented automobiles, and public buses. You travel through the verdant Naxian countryside on the picturesque journey.

Church of Panagia Filotitissa: The majestic Panagia Filotitissa Church is the focal point of Filoti. This Byzantine cathedral honoring the Virgin Mary has stunning murals and striking architecture. Explore the interior at your leisure and savor the tranquil ambiance.

Village Square and Cafés: Traditional white-washed buildings encircle Filoti's central square, making for a picturesque scene. The area is dotted with cafés and tavernas, offering a great place to have a tasty meal or a Greek coffee while soaking up the atmosphere of the neighborhood.

Olive Oil Museum: Visit the Olive Oil Museum in Filoti to discover more about the abundant olive oil production of Naxos. The museum provides a fascinating look into a crucial component of Naxian agriculture by showcasing the history and customs around the extraction of olive oil.

Aria Spring: The Aria Spring is a natural water source surrounded by beautiful greenery that is accessible after a short stroll from Filoti. It's a peaceful place to unwind, take in the scenery, and maybe have a picnic.

Craftsmanship of Naxian Marble: You may see the island's marble workmanship in Filoti, which is well-known for its marble quarries. Investigate the neighborhood's workshops and studios where artists produce exquisite marble goods and sculptures.

Folklore Museum of Filoti: Visit this museum to learn more about the history and culture of the Naxian people. The museum offers insight into the agricultural life of the island by showcasing traditional items, clothes, and equipment.

Village Walks and Hikes: There are hiking trails all around Filoti that lead to picturesque vistas and nearby villages. Take a stroll in the countryside to take in the scenery and historical sites.

Local Cuisine: Filoti offers good opportunities for sampling traditional Naxian cuisine. The village's tavern serves food prepared with regional ingredients, including dairy, beef, and fresh vegetables.

Agia Kyriaki Monastery: Take a tour of the adjacent Agia Kyriaki Monastery, which is perched on Mount Zas. For those interested in historical and religious sites, the monastery is a worthwhile visit because it provides sweeping views of Filoti and the surrounding surroundings.

Practical Tips: Filoti's height might result in lower temperatures, especially in the nights, so it's advised to pack a light jacket or sweater. In case you want to go around the village, make sure your shoes are comfy.

Discovering the culture, taking in the scenery, and experiencing real village living all come together beautifully during a day tour to Filoti Village. Filoti provides a typical Naxian experience, whether you're interested in history, trekking, or enjoying the regional cuisine.

CHAPTER TWELVE: PRACTICAL INFORMATION

Currency and Banking

Similar to the rest of Greece, currency and banking in Naxos are governed by the Euro (€). Here is a thorough resource for travelers visiting Naxos on money, banking options, and financial matters:

Currency: Greece's official currency since 2001 has been the Euro (€). There are 100 pennies in every Euro. The fact that coins and banknotes are available in a variety of denominations facilitates the exchange of different values.

Banking Services: Visitors can obtain banking services at a number of banks and ATMs (Automated Teller Machines) on Naxos, especially in Naxos Town. There are branches of several of the country's largest banks on the island, including National Bank of Greece, Alpha Bank, and Piraeus Bank.

ATMs: Naxos Town and a few larger villages have plenty of ATMs. Visitors can use foreign credit or debit cards to withdraw euros from there. Before leaving, make sure your card will function overseas and ask your bank about any possible fees.

Credit Cards: Visa and Mastercard are the most generally accepted credit cards in Naxos, particularly at tourist-oriented businesses, hotels, and larger restaurants. Cash, however, might be the favored mode of payment in smaller towns or more isolated locations.

Exchange of Currencies: - Although the main places to get Euros are banks and ATMs, there can be some currency exchange offices nearby, especially in tourist destinations. On the other hand, better rates are typically offered when converting money at banks or ATMs.

Visitor's Checks:- The increased availability of ATMs has led to a decrease in the use of traveler's checks. For convenience, using a combination of cash and cards is advised.

Bank Holidays: Greece's banking hours typically adhere to a set timetable. Generally, banks are open from 8:00 AM to 2:30 PM, Monday through Thursday, and from 8:00 AM to 2:00 PM on Fridays. Remember that these times could change, so it's best to find out the precise hours of operation for the branch you want to visit.

Currency Advice: It's a good idea to have some cash on hand for transactions at markets, cafes, or other local establishments that might only accept cash payments. This is especially true for lower denominations.

- To ensure that using your cards overseas won't cause any problems, let your bank know when and where you plan to travel.

- Remember that not all places will accept traveler's checks, so it's best to have a variety of payment choices.

Because there are many ATMs and cards are accepted, handling money and banking in Naxos is usually simple. On the other hand, having cash on hand and being aware of your bank's policies can help to guarantee a hassle-free financial trip to the island.

Local Customs

Like many other Greek islands, Naxos has a diverse range of regional traditions that pay homage to its historical and cultural background. Respecting and being aware of these traditions improves your stay and encourages goodwill among the locals. This is a thorough overview to some of the Naxos local traditions:

1. Salutations and Courtesies: Greetings are very important to Greeks. Greetings often begin with a firm handshake. It is considered polite to address persons with "Mr." or "Mrs." followed by their last name because politeness is highly appreciated.

2. Smacking Both Cheeks: When saying hello or goodbye, it's customary for friends and family to plant kisses on both cheeks. This gesture implies warmth and connection. Men may also greet each other with a pat on the back or a handshake.

3. Serving Food and Beverages: Greeks are renowned for being welcoming. It is usual to bring a little gift, such as pastries or a bottle of wine, if you are welcomed to someone's house. In order to emphasize plenty and generosity, hosts frequently require that visitors assist themselves for seconds at events.

4. Regarding Spiritual Traditions: Greek society places a high value on religion. When visiting cathedrals or monasteries, it's important to dress modestly, covering shoulders and knees. Locals engage in processions and church services during religious festivities, and outsiders are expected to observe discreetly.

5. Classic Music and Dancing: Greeks use ancient dances and music to commemorate major occasions and show their enthusiasm. Do not hesitate to participate in a dance if you are invited. Your excitement will be appreciated by the locals, even if you're not familiar with the steps.

6. Table Etiquette: It is traditional to wait to eat during meals until the host says "kalí óreksi" (excellent appetite). Completing everything on your plate is a sign of good manners and meal enjoyment. After eating, it's customary for the locals to stay at the table and have conversations.

7. Festivals and festivities: Throughout the year, Naxos holds a number of festivals and festivities, many of which are connected to religious activities. If you happen to be on the island during one of these holidays, join in the festivities to experience the colorful local culture.

8. Giving and Getting Assistance: Greeks are renowned for their altruistic nature. Never be afraid to seek help from a local if you're lost or in need. Similarly, it is valued when you offer assistance to someone in need.

9. Tradition of Siesta: In Naxos, having a quick siesta in the afternoon is still a widespread custom. In the early afternoon, a lot of stores and establishments could close, particularly in smaller settlements. Make appropriate plans for your activities and accept that life moves more slowly during these hours.

10. Local Slang and Expressions: Even though English is the primary language in tourist regions, the people there value visitors who try to pick up a few simple Greek phrases. "Kalimera" means "good morning," "Kalispera" means "good evening," and "Efharisto" means "thank you."

One of the most important aspects of cultural immersion and fostering strong relationships with the locals in Naxos is respecting customs. Respecting the customs, taking part in the festivities, and acting politely all contribute to making this lovely Greek island an unforgettable and respectful experience.

Emergency Contacts

It's critical to know who to contact in case of emergency when visiting Naxos in order to protect your safety and wellbeing. This is a thorough list of Naxos's key emergency contacts:

1. General Emergency Services - Phone Number: 112 - The emergency number 112 can be used for general emergencies. This number connects you to a range of agencies, including fire, police, and ambulance. English-speaking operators are available.

2. Medical Emergencies:- Ambulance: 166 - Contact the ambulance service in the event of a medical emergency. They'll take you to the closest hospital or clinic.

3. Police: - Police Station (Naxos Town):+30 22850 22100

The local police station in Naxos Town can help with a number of things, including reporting occurrences or requesting assistance.

4. Tourist Police: - Tourist Police (Naxos Town): +30 22850 22100 They can offer assistance with misplaced documents, information, and other tourist-related problems.

The Tourist Police are specially trained to help visitors.

5. Fire Department: - Fire Department (Naxos Town): +30 22850 22444

In case of a fire, get in touch with the nearby fire department. They have received training in managing fires and similar events.

6. Coast Guard (Naxos Town): +30 22850 23043 - Coast Guard: In addition to being in charge of maritime safety, the Coast Guard can help with crises involving the sea.

7. Pharmacies:- Pharmacies are crucial if you require prescription drugs or medical advice. In Naxos, the majority of pharmacies are open during regular business hours. In the event that a pharmacy is closed, information regarding the closest open pharmacy is typically posted on the door.

8. Hospitals and Medical Centers: - Health Center of Filoti: +30 22850 31221 - Naxos General Hospital (Naxos Town): +30 22850 23145 - These medical facilities are capable of offering emergency medical care. The primary medical facility on the island is the hospital located in Naxos Town.

9. Veterinary Services: The veterinary clinic in Naxos Town can be reached at +30 22850 26018. This Naxos Town clinic can help with veterinarian treatment if you are traveling with dogs and need assistance for their medical needs.

10. Off-road Support: There are various roadside help services accessible if you have automotive trouble. For assistance or information about nearby services, get in touch with your rental car provider.

11. Consulates and Embassies If you are a visitor from abroad, make sure to know the address and phone number of the embassy or consulate of your nation in Greece. They can help with a number of problems, such as emergency or misplaced passports.

Mountain Rescue (Naxos): +30 22850 23875 - Having the phone number of mountain rescue services on hand is crucial if you intend to partake in any mountain activities, like hiking.

Make sure your phone has the local numbers saved, and if you're taking a cell phone from abroad, make sure it can make international calls if necessary. If you're staying in a more isolated part of the island, get to know the whereabouts of hospitals and police stations, among other important services. A safer and more pleasurable trip to Naxos is enhanced by being organized and knowledgeable about emergency contacts.

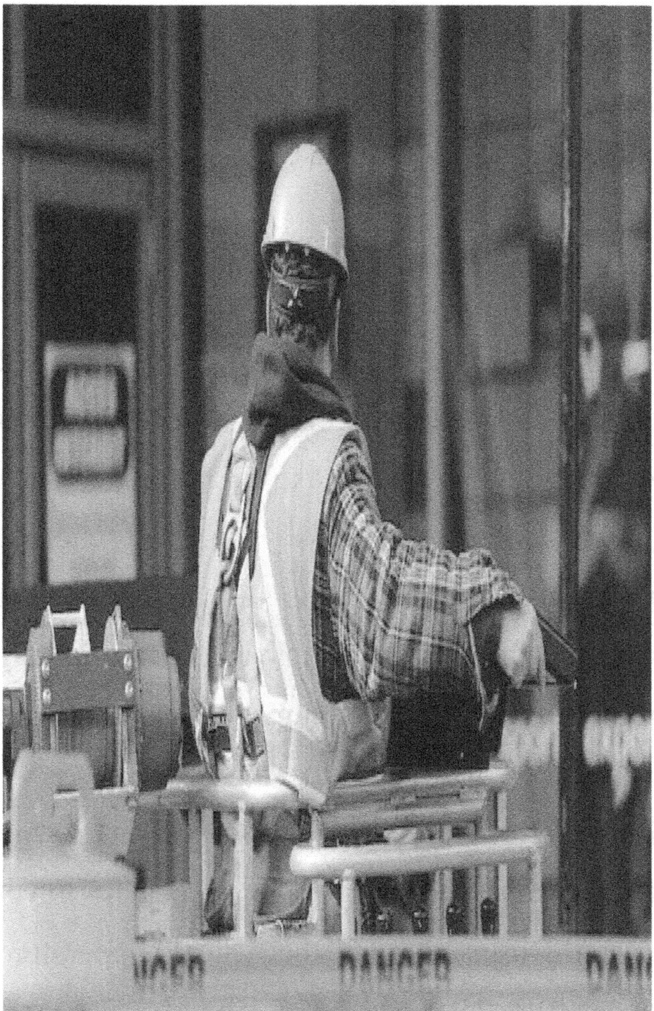
DANGER

CHAPTER THIRTEEN: USEFUL TIPS

Best Time to Visit

Depending on your interests and the kind of experience you're looking for, there is no set optimal time to visit Naxos. Like many other Greek islands, Naxos has a year-round schedule of events and attractions. To assist you in choosing the ideal time to visit, the following provides a thorough summary of the various seasons:

Summertime (June to August): Summer, with its hot, dry weather, is Naxos' busiest travel season. During the day, the typical temperature ranges from 25°C to 35°C (77°F to 95°F).

Activities: For those who enjoy the beach and the ocean, this is the perfect moment. The glistening seas are ideal for aquatic sports like swimming and snorkeling. Summertime is a time for a lot of outdoor activities, festivals, and cultural events.

Autumn (September to October) and Spring (April to May): Mild temperatures are seen in the spring and fall, with daytime highs between 18°C and 28°C (64°F and 82°F). The weather is pleasant for outdoor activities throughout these seasons.

Activities: The best seasons to explore the island's scenery, hiking routes, and historical monuments are in the spring and fall. It's still nice to swim in the sea, and there aren't as many people there as during the height of summer. With its verdant surroundings and blossoming flowers, springtime is especially beautiful.

3. Cold season (November through March): The winter months in Naxos are colder, with daytime highs between 10°C and 16°C (50°F and 61°F). This is the season when it rains most frequently.

Activities: Winter can be a tranquil time to enjoy the local way of life, even if it is not the busiest travel season. During this time, certain establishments catering to tourists may close, but Naxos still has its own unique appeal. Winter is a good time to visit if you want to be more reflective and quiet.

Aspects to Take Into Account: - **Crowds:** If you'd rather have a more sedate experience and want to stay away from big groups, think about going during the shoulder seasons (autumn or spring).

Spending Plan: Off-peak seasons typically have lower lodging and travel costs. It can be less expensive to travel in the spring or the fall.

Preferences for Weather: Summer is the finest season if you like being outside in the heat and at the beach. The best seasons to explore the outdoors and enjoy warmer weather are spring and fall.

Special Events:- June to September: Naxos Festival This cultural festival provides a distinctive summertime cultural experience by showcasing theater, dance, and music performances.

August 15 is Apollolonia Feast Day: This religious feast is observed all throughout the island and is marked by processions, traditional music, and celebrations.

Final Analysis: The ideal time to go to Naxos will depend on your interests and the kind of experience you're looking for. Naxos has lots to offer all year round, whether you like the exuberant energy of summer, the flowering landscapes of spring, or the peace of fall and winter. To get the most of this stunning Greek island, decide what your top priorities are and arrange your stay accordingly.

Packing Essentials

Packing necessities before your vacation to Naxos will help you be ready for the wide range of activities and weather conditions on the island. Here is a thorough list of things to think about:

- Clothes: For the warm weather, wear airy and lightweight items like summer dresses, T-shirts, and shorts.Swimwear for trips to the beach.cozy walking shoes for hiking trails and village explorationFor sun protection, use a hat and sunglasses.For chilly evenings, especially in the spring or fall, wear a

light jacket or sweater.Modest clothes for trips to churches and religious sites.
- Travel Documents:Passport or ID card.documentation for travel insurance.Reservations for travel and lodging.Important document copy (separately preserved).
- Health and Personal Care: A basic first aid kit containing bandages, analgesics, and any prescription drugs that may be requiredHigh SPF sun protection.Nighttime insect repellant things for personal hygiene.
- Electronics and Chargers:Universal adapter for charging electronic devices.Using a smartphone or camera to record memories portable power bank to keep electronics charged.

- Cash and Payment: Enough cash for petty purchases and in case you come across locations that don't take credit or debit cards.Credit/debit cards, advising your bank of your travel dates.
- 6. Beach bag or daypack: A compact daypack for bringing necessities on walks or day excursions.Bring a beach bag, sunscreen, a good book, and a blanket for your beach adventures.
- Reusable Water Bottle: Drink plenty of water, particularly on hot summer days.
- Snorkeling Gear: If you're like snorkeling, bring your own mask and snorkel to explore the underwater beauty of Naxos' beaches.
- Reusable Water Bottle: Bring a reusable water bottle to refill throughout your adventures.

- Maps and Guidebook: Use a map or guidebook to tour Naxos and find hidden treasures.
- Light Rain Jacket: —Even if it doesn't rain often in the summer, it's still a good idea to bring one, particularly if you're traveling in the spring or fall.
- Comfy Daypack or Backpack: - A daypack or backpack that is suitable for hiking or day trips, with ample room for necessities and items that you may find while exploring.
- Quick-Dry Towel: A quick-dry towel dries quicker than a standard towel and is particularly helpful on beach days.
- Reusable Shopping Bag: - A little reusable bag is useful for holding groceries or trinkets.

- Respectful attire: - Modest attire for visits to religious sites or local villages, particularly if you wish to explore churches.
- Power Strip: - If you have many gadgets to charge, a travel-sized power strip can be useful.
- Dry Bag: - If you're going to be doing any water sports, make sure your valuables are dry.
- Adapters and Converters: - Bring the appropriate adapters and converters if the plug types on your electronic gadgets change.
- Travel Locks: - Locks to protect your valuables or bags.Keep in mind that Naxos is a laid-back destination, so you don't need to bring too much. Adapt your packing list to your own schedule and

tastes, and you'll be ready to take advantage of everything Naxos has to offer.

Safety Tips

When visiting Naxos, it is crucial to make sure you are safe. Although most people think the island is safe, it's still important to pay attention to your surroundings and abide by basic safety precautions. An extensive list of safety advice for your trip to Naxos is provided here:

1. Safety of Swimming:
- Swim only in places that are approved and secure.
- Be mindful of the currents and the weather.
- Pay attention to any flags or warnings on the beaches.

- Seek guidance from lifeguards or locals if you're not familiar with the area's waters.

2. Sun Protection:
- Use a high-SPF sunscreen to shield your skin from the intense Mediterranean sun.
- For extra sun protection, wear hats, sunglasses, and light clothing.
- Drink lots of water to stay hydrated, especially on hot summer days.

3. Health Precautions:
- Always have a basic first aid kit and the essential drugs on hand.
- Avoid heat-related ailments and stay hydrated.
- If you are experiencing a medical emergency, call the nearest hospital or the local emergency number, 112, for assistance.

4. Road Safety:
- Drive carefully and cross roads with caution.
- Observe traffic laws and keep in mind that certain places may have narrow or curving roads.
- When renting a car, be sure you have the required papers and drive carefully.

5. Mountain Safety:
- Let someone know your plans if you're going on a hike or exploring a mountainous location.
- Always keep an eye on your surroundings, follow designated paths, and carry a map.
- Wear comfortable attire and sturdy shoes when engaging in outside activities.

6. Respect Local Customs:

- Pay attention to regional traditions and customs, particularly while you're at places of worship.
- When required, dress modestly, and abide with any rules posted in places of worship or culture.

7. Water Activities:
- Make sure you are supervised by knowledgeable instructors or guides when participating in water sports or activities.
- Use suitable safety equipment, such as life jackets, as necessary.

8. Emergency Contacts:
- Store important emergency contacts on your phone, such as the local emergency number, the embassy or consulate of your nation, and the specifics of your lodging.

9. Beware of Scams:
- Keep an eye out for dishonest or unduly pushy sellers.
- Be wary of unsolicited offers and use reliable agencies for tours and activities.

10. Drink Responsibly:
- Use alcohol in moderation and pay attention to your surroundings, particularly in busy places or places with a vibrant nightlife.
- Keep an eye on your beverage to avoid any possible manipulation.

11. Protect Valuables: Avoid flaunting pricey items in public and keep valuables safe.
- Keep additional cash, passports, and important documents secure in hotel safes.
- Make sure you have comprehensive travel insurance that covers medical

emergencies, trip cancellations, and lost possessions.

12. Awareness of Weather:
- Keep up with the weather, particularly if you're planning an outdoor activity.
- Take into account the temperature and any anticipated weather changes while planning outdoor activities.

13. Remain Updated:
- Throughout your visit, be abreast of local news and any advisories regarding travel.

You may minimize dangers and maximize your overall experience in Naxos by adhering to these safety precautions. Recall that adopting the required safety precautions, being mindful of your surroundings, and honoring local traditions all help to make your trip to the island safer and more enjoyable.

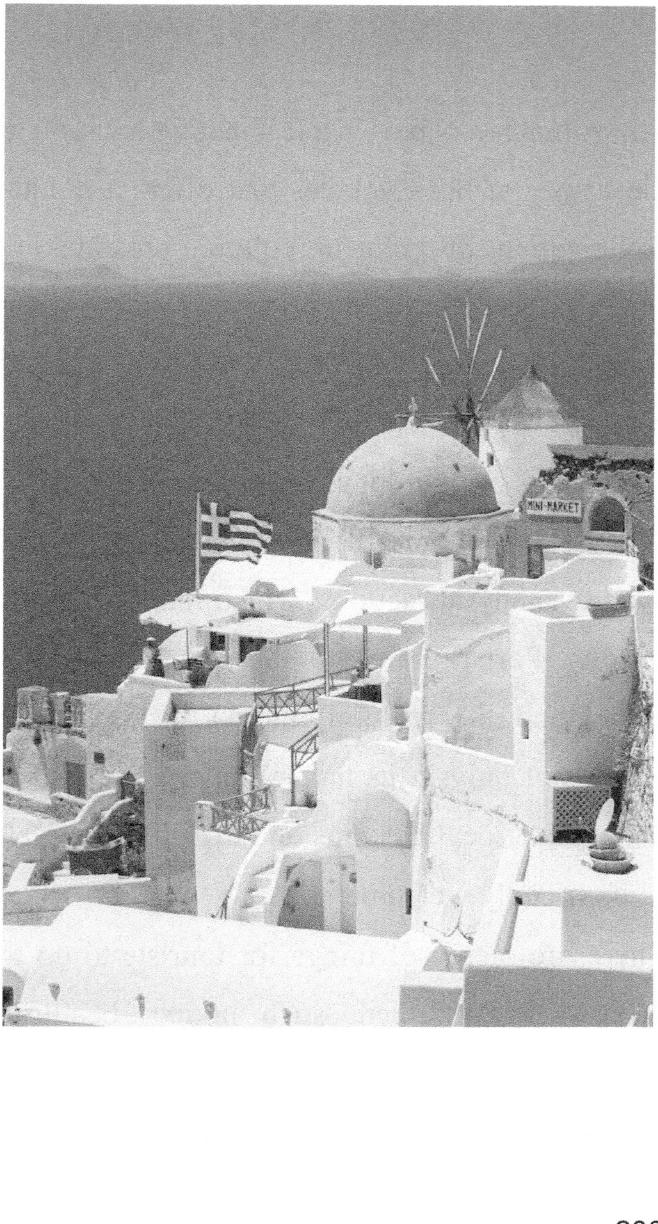
MINI-MARKET

CONCLUSION

In summary, Naxos is a fascinating location in the center of the Cyclades that offers a unique combination of colorful culture, breathtaking scenery, and a deep history. Naxos offers something for every kind of traveler, whether it's its immaculate beaches, historical attractions, or traditional towns that entice you.

A well-rounded experience is offered by the island's many attractions, which range from the historic Portara ruins to the quaint alleys of Chora and the tranquil interior vistas. Naxos excels not only in its natural beauty but also in its genuine local customs and traditions, as well as its friendly welcome.

There are plenty of things for tourists to do to keep them occupied, such hiking, beautiful trails, swimming, water sports, and just relaxing on the golden beaches. The island's appeal is enhanced by the festivals and cultural events that take place all year long and provide tourists an opportunity to fully experience local culture.

Well-connected transportation, a wide range of lodging choices, and a variety of dining establishments offering mouthwatering regional cuisine all make it easy to navigate Naxos. Whether you're looking for a quiet break in the middle of nature, a family-friendly vacation, or a vibrant nightlife scene, the island has something to offer everyone.

Naxos emerges as a tapestry of relaxation and exploration, from the breathtaking vistas from Mount Zas to the charming towns of Chalki and Apiranthos. For those who are ready to explore beyond the main island, the Small Cyclades beckon with even more hidden beauties to be discovered on day trips.

Naxos awaits you with wide arms, whether you prefer the vibrant summer energy, the blossoming spring sceneries, or the more sedate autumn and winter atmosphere. Discovering Naxos, with its cobblestone streets, blue waters, and regional cuisine, makes it clear that this is a place that will always hold a special place in the hearts of travelers.

When planning your trip to Naxos, take into account the many options available from this Greek treasure; every season has its own distinct charm. Accept the past of the island, become involved in the rituals of the people, and enjoy the beauty that makes Naxos an enduring gem of the Aegean. Naxos awaits you whether you're a culture vulture, a passionate traveler, or someone looking for peace and quiet. It promises an experience that will stay with you long after your trip is over.

Recap of Highlights

When we go over the attractions of Naxos, it becomes clear that this Greek island is a treasure with many facets and a wide variety of experiences. The following are the main features that render Naxos an enthralling destination:

- Celebrities of History:- Explore the ancient ruins of the Portara, a gigantic marble entrance that stands as a symbol of Naxos. Explore the Temple of Apollo and other ruins to get a taste of the island's colorful history.
- Villages with Charm: Explore the charming streets of Chora, the capital of Naxos, with its vibrant squares, tavernas, and Venetian architecture. Explore historic communities with distinct

personalities and cultural allure, such as Apiranthos and Chalki.

- Stunning Beaches: Indulge in the sun-soaked beauty of Naxos' beaches. From the wide sands of Plaka to the crystal-clear waters of Agios Prokopios, the island features some of the most pristine and scenic beaches in the Aegean.
- Cultural Celebrations and Events:Attend events like the Naxos Festival, where theater, dance, and music acts take place against the backdrop of historic venues, to fully immerse yourself in the rich local culture. Participate in customary events such as the Apollonia Feast to experience a genuine flavor of regional festivities.

- Nature Scenes: Explore Naxos' interior, where lush terrain, fruitful valleys, and olive orchards create a picturesque scene. Climb Mount Zas, the Cyclades' highest mountain, for expansive vistas and an exhilarating experience.
- Culinary Delights: Naxian cuisine, renowned for its traditional flavors and fresh ingredients, will delight your taste buds. Savor regional specialties at coastal tavernas, such as graviera cheese, Kitron liqueur, and delicious fish.
- Day Trips to the Small Cyclades: Go on day trips to the Small Cyclades and explore the pristine beauty of islands such as Koufonisia, Schinoussa, and Iraklia. These trips provide a peaceful diversion from the busy main island.

- Byzantine and Venetian Heritage: Marvel at the Byzantine architecture of churches like Panagia Drossiani and the Venetian influence found in the Kastro of Naxos Town. These old buildings shed light on the rich cultural legacy of the island.
- Naxian artistry: Witness the island's artistry, from marble carving in Apollonas to local artists producing handmade items. Take mementos home that showcase Naxos' genuine artistic talent.
- Sports and Leisure: Naxos offers a variety of recreational activities, including trekking beautiful paths, enjoying water sports, and relaxing on its beaches. There are activities for all kinds of travelers on the island thanks to its varied settings.

- Warm warmth: Experience the genuine warmth of the natives. Because Naxians are renowned for being kind and warm-hearted, the entire vacation experience is improved by their welcoming attitude.

Naxos, then, captures the spirit of the Aegean, a symphony of natural beauty, history, and cultural diversity. Naxos is an island that begs to be explored, offering both historical wonders and contemporary pleasures. It also promises life-changing experiences and a close bond with the Cyclades' core.

Farewell to Naxos

Naxos leaves you with treasured memories and a deep connection to its singular fusion of history, culture, and scenic beauty as you say goodbye. This is a thorough analysis of the final goodbye to Naxos:

1. Contemplating Past Events: Think for a moment about the variety of experiences Naxos has to offer. Every minute of your Naxian adventure, whether you're discovering historic ruins, meandering through charming villages, or relaxing on immaculate beaches, adds to the overall image.

2. Cultural Appreciation: Take in the rich cultural mosaic of Naxos, from its colorful local customs to its Byzantine and Venetian heritage. Greek island life is forever changed by the island's festivals, traditional music, and gracious hospitality.

3. Establishment with Locals: The island's distinct appeal is influenced by the Naxian people's sincere warmth and kindness. The relationships made with locals—whether via

simple conversations, shared experiences, or traditional meals—become enduring memories.

4. Farewell to Natural Beauty: Say goodbye to the breathtaking scenery that characterizes Naxos, including its beaches' golden sands, its interior's emerald hues, and its mountain peaks' expansive views. Enjoy one last look at the captivating sunsets that create a kaleidoscope of colors in the sky.

5.Stories from the Kitchen: Savor the tastes of Naxian cuisine that have tantalize your palate. The culinary delights of the island leave a lasting impression on your palette and emotions, whether it's the regional cheeses, exquisite seafood, or the sweet undertones of Kitron liqueur.

6. Reflection of the Small Cyclades: If you visited the Small Cyclades, consider the peace and pristine beauty of these lesser-known

treasures. The day tours to islands like Iraklia and Koufonisia enhance your farewell with a feeling of adventure and exploration.

7. Cobblestone alleyways and coastal Tavernas: Recall the beauty of roaming around Naxos' cobblestone alleyways, discovering secret corners in villages, and savoring meals at coastal tavernas. These moments perfectly capture the island's laid-back vibe and genuine pace.

8. Drawing to a Close with Panoramas: Bid farewell to the broad views that welcomed you from the cliffs of the Kastro, the summit of Mount Zas, or the picturesque overlooks. The spirit of the many landscapes of Naxos is captured in these viewpoints.

9. Thank You for the Hospitality: Express your appreciation for the Naxian people's kind hospitality. A feeling of community is fostered

by the residents' hospitality and desire to share their island with guests, which persists long after you say goodbye.

10. Return Promise: As you leave Naxos, carry with you the promise of return. The charm of the island and the memories it has given you are a call to return and explore more of its undiscovered areas.

11. Goodbye, Sunset: Think about taking in a final sunset, maybe from your favorite spot. Let the sunset and the sky's hues represent a magnificent end to your Naxian journey.

You will carry the spirit of Naxos with you when you set off on your trip away from it. It's not a farewell, but rather a "see you later," with the possibility of revisiting this captivating Aegean gem in the future.

Made in United States
Orlando, FL
03 February 2024